Melody, Lyrics and Simplifie

MW00564327

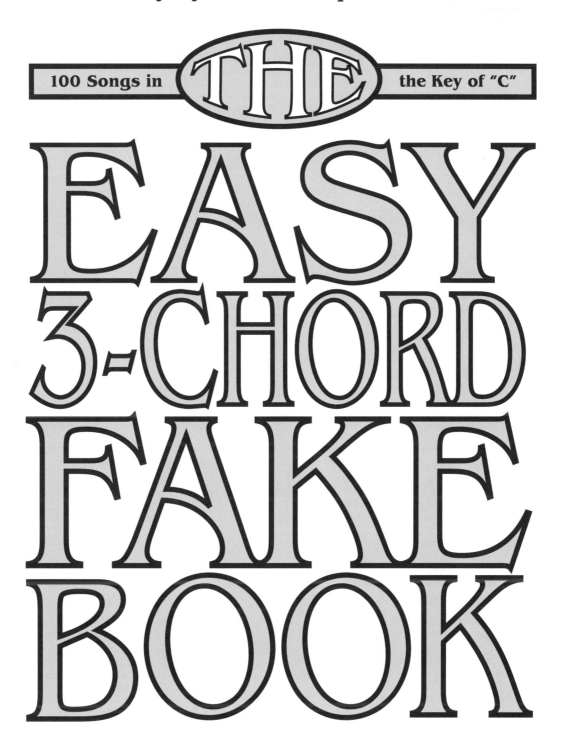

100 Songs in **THE** the Key of "C"

EASY
3-CHORD
FAKE
BOOK

ISBN 978-1-4584-0541-8

HAL•LEONARD®
CORPORATION

7777 W. BLUEMOUND RD. P.O. BOX 13819 MILWAUKEE, WI 53213

Visit Hal Leonard Online at
www.halleonard.com

THE EASY 3-CHORD FAKE BOOK

CONTENTS

INTRODUCTION

What Is a Fake Book?

A fake book has one-line music notation consisting of melody, lyrics and chord symbols. This lead sheet format is a "musical shorthand" which is an invaluable resource for all musicians—hobbyists to professionals.

Here's how *The Easy 3-Chord Fake Book* differs from most standard fake books:

- All songs are in the key of C.

- Only three basic chord types are used—major, minor and seventh.

- The music notation is larger for ease of reading.

In the event that you haven't used chord symbols to create accompaniment, or your experience is limited, a chord speller chart is included at the back of the book to help you get started.

Have fun!

AMANDA

Words and Music by
BOB McDILL

AIN'T NO SUNSHINE

Words and Music by
BILL WITHERS

Slow Blues-Rock feel

Ain't no sun-shine when she's gone. It's not warm when she's a-

way. Ain't no sun-shine when she's gone, _____ and she's al-ways gone too

long an-y-time she goes a-way. Won-der this time where she's

gone,
gone,
won-der if she's gone to stay.
on - ly dark-ness ev-'ry day.
Ain't no sun-shine when she's

To Coda

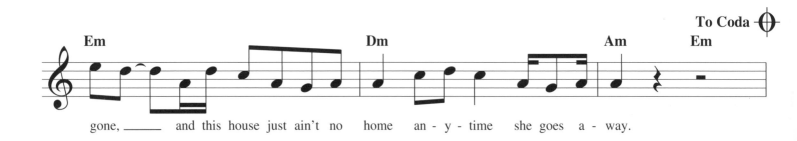

gone, _____ and this house just ain't no home an-y-time she goes a-way.

And I know, I know, I know, I know, I know, I know, I know, I know, __ I know, I

know, I know, I know, __ I know, I know, I know, I know, I know, I know, I know, I know,

I know, I know, I know, I know, I know, I know, hey, __ I ought to leave the young thing a-

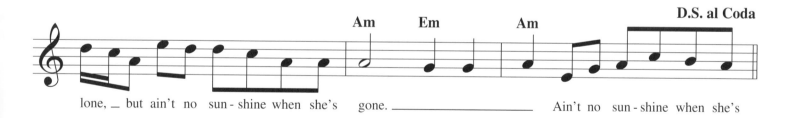

lone, __ but ain't no sun-shine when she's gone. _____ Ain't no sun-shine when she's

An - y - time __ she goes a - way.

ALL SHOOK UP

Words and Music by OTIS BLACKWELL
and ELVIS PRESLEY

Moderate Shuffle

A - well - a, bless my soul. ___ What's wrong with me? ___ I'm
hands are shak - y and my knees are weak, I

itch - ing like a man ___ on a fuz - zy tree. ___ My friends say I'm act - in'
can't ___ seem to stand ___ on my own two feet. ___ Who do you thank when you

queer as a bug, ___ I'm in love. ⎫
have ___ such luck? ___ I'm in love. ⎭ I'm all shook up! ___ Mm ___

mm oh, oh yeah, ___ yeah! _____ My

yeah! _____ Please don't ask what's ___ on my mind. ___ I'm a
tongue gets tied when I try to speak. ___ My ___

lit - tle mixed up but I'm feel - in' fine. ___ When I'm near that girl that
in - sides shake like a leaf on a tree. There's ___ only one cure for this

9

ALL TOGETHER NOW

Words and Music by JOHN LENNON
and PAUL McCARTNEY

Moderately

One, two, three, four, can I have __ a lit - tle more? __

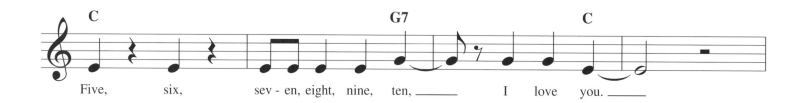

Five, six, sev - en, eight, nine, ten, ____ I love you. ____

A, B, C, D, can I bring __ my friend to tea? __

E, F, G, H, I, ____ J, ____ I love you. __ (Bom, bom, bom, bom - pa bom)

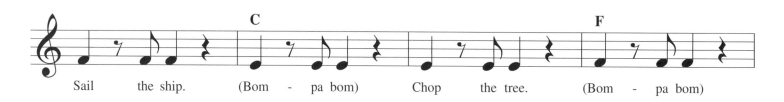

Sail the ship. (Bom - pa bom) Chop the tree. (Bom - pa bom)

To Coda ⊕

Skip the rope. (Bom - pa bom) Look at me! ____ (All to-geth-er now)

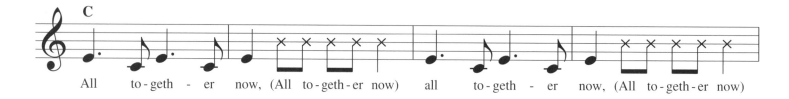

All to-geth - er now, (All to-geth-er now) all to-geth - er now, (All to-geth-er now)

AMERICAN WOMAN

Written by BURTON CUMMINGS, RANDY BACHMAN,
GARY PETERSON and JIM KALE

Moderately slow

A - mer - i - can wom - an, _____ gon - na mess your mind. _____

A - mer - i - can wom - an, she gon - na mess your mind. _____

A - mer - i - can wom - an, _____ gon - na mess your mind. _____

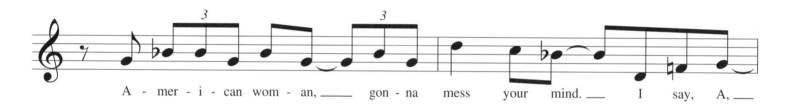

A - mer - i - can wom - an, _____ gon - na mess your mind. _____ I say, A, _____

_____ I say M, _____ I say E, _____ I say R, _____

_____ say I, _____ use C, _____ say A, _____

_____ N. _____ A - mer - i - can wom - an, _____ gon - na

mess your mind. ___   A - mer - i - can wom - an, ___ gon - na mess your mind. ___

A - mer - i - can wom - an, ___ gon - na mess your mind. ___

(Instrumental)

C

1. A - mer - i - can wom - - an, stay a-way from me, ___ A - mer - i - can wom -
2.,3. *(See additional lyrics)*

- an, ma-ma, let me be. ___ Don't come hang-in' a - round ___ my door, ___

I don't wan - na see your face ___ no more. I got more im - por - tant things to do ___ than

spend my time ___ grow-in' old with you. ___ Now, wom - an, I said stay a - way. ___

bye. _____ You're __ no good __ for me. __ I'm no good for you. __

Gon-na look you right in the eye, __ tell you what I'm gon-na do. __ You know I'm gon-na

C

leave. You know I'm gon - na go. You know I'm gon - na

Vocal ad lib.

Repeat and Fade

leave. I know I'm gon - na go, _____ wom - an. I'm gon-na...

Additional Lyrics

2. American woman, get away from me
American woman, mama, let me be
Don't wanna see your shadow no more
Colored lights can hypnotize
Sparkle someone else's eyes
Now, woman, I said get away
American woman, listen what I say.

3. American woman, said get away
American woman, listen what I say
Don't come hangin' around my door
Don't wanna see your face no more
I don't need your war machines
I don't need your ghetto scenes
Colored lights can hypnotize
Sparkle someone else's eyes
Now, woman, get away from me
American woman, mama, let me be.

BAD CASE OF LOVING YOU

Words and Music by
JOHN MOON MARTIN

Moderate Rock

Hot sum-mer night. _____ Fell like a net; I got-ta
_____ don't make no pret-ty heart. _ I learned
_____ twen-ty-one to zip; a smile of

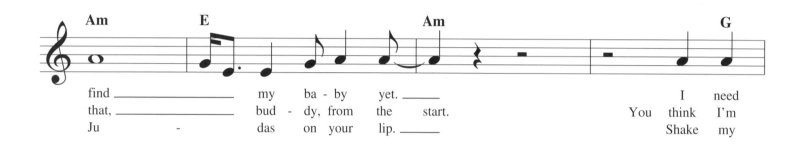

find _____ my ba-by yet. _____ I need
that, _____ bud-dy, from the start. You think I'm
Ju - das on your lip. _____ Shake my

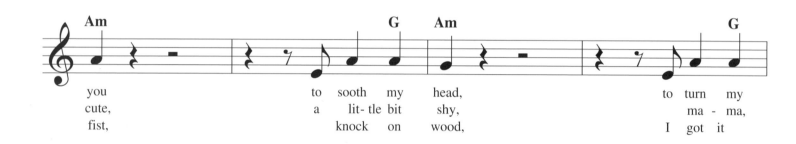

you to sooth my head, to turn my
cute, a lit-tle bit shy, ma - ma,
fist, knock on wood, I got it

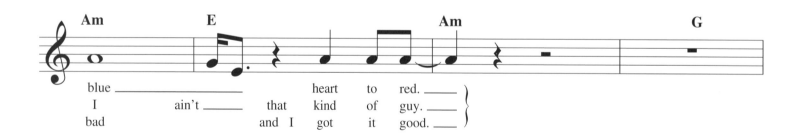

blue _____ heart to red. _____
I ain't _____ that kind of guy. _____
bad and I got it good. _____

N.C.

Doc-tor, doc - tor, give me the news. _ I got a bad case of lov-in' you. _____

No pill's gon-na cure my ill. ___ I got a bad case of lov - in' you. _

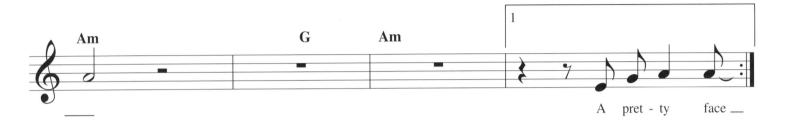

___ A pret - ty face ___

I know you like ___ it, you like it on

top. Tell me, ma - ma, are you gon - na stop. _

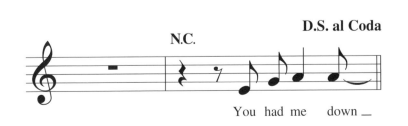

You had me down _

___

THE BALLAD OF JOHN AND YOKO

Words and Music by JOHN LENNON
and PAUL McCARTNEY

Moderate Rock

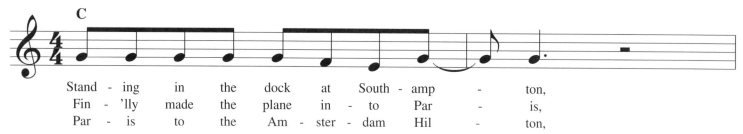

Stand - ing in the dock at South - amp - ton,
Fin - 'lly made the plane in - to Par - is,
Par - is to the Am - ster - dam Hil - ton,

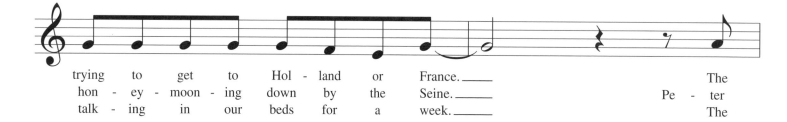

trying to get to Hol - land or France._____ The
hon - ey - moon - ing down by the Seine._____ Pe - ter
talk - ing in our beds for a week._____ The

man in the mac_____ said,_____ "You've got to go back."_____ You know they
Brown called to say,_____ "You_____ can make it O - K._____ You can get
news - peo - ple said,_____ "Say, what're you do - ing in bed?"_____ I said, "We're

did - n't e - ven give us a chance._____
mar - ried in Gi - bral - tar, near Spain."_____ } Christ! You know it ain't eas-
on - ly trying to get us some peace."_____

- y,_____ you know how hard it can be._____

The way things are go - ing,_____

they're gon - na cru - ci - fy_____ me. (*Instrumental*)

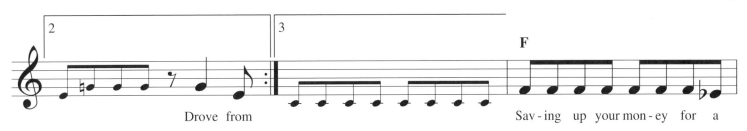

Drove from

Sav - ing up your mon - ey for a

rain - y day, _____ giv - ing all your clothes to char - i -

ty. Last night the wife said, "Oh boy, when you're dead, you

don't take noth - ing with you but your soul." _____ Think!

Made a light - ning trip to Vi - en - na,
Caught the ear - ly plane back to Lon - don,

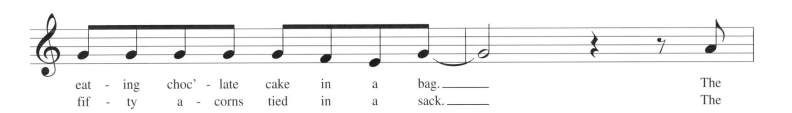

eat - ing choc' - late cake in a bag. ____ The
fif - ty a - corns tied in a sack. ____ The

news - pa - pers said, _____ "She's gone to his head; _____ they
men from the press ____ said, ____ "We wish you suc - cess; _____ it's

BARBARA ANN

Words and Music by
FRED FASSERT

Bright Rock tempo

(Bar - bar Ann, Bar - bar - bar Ann, Bar - bar Ann, Bar - bar - bar Ann.) Bar - bar

Ann, _____ take ___ my hand. _____ Bar - bar

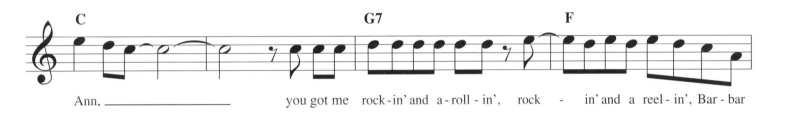

Ann, _____ you got me rock-in' and a-roll-in', rock - in' and a reel-in', Bar - bar

Ann, Bar - bar - bar - bar - bar Ann. Went to a dance, look-in' for ro - mance,
Tried Bet - ty Lou, tried Peg - gy Sue,

saw Bar - bar Ann, so I thought I take a chance. Oh, Bar - bar Ann, Bar - bar Ann,
danced with Mar - y Lou, but I knew they would-n't do.

take my hand. Oh, Bar - bar Ann, _____ take my hand. You got me

**2nd time
D.C. al Fine**

rock - in' and a-roll-in', rock - in' and a reel - in', Bar - bar Ann, Bar - bar - bar - bar - bar Ann.

BE-BOP-A-LULA

Words and Music by TEX DAVIS
and GENE VINCENT

Moderately slow Rock

Be - bop - a - lu - la, she's my ba - by. Be - bop - a - lu - la, I don't mean may - be.

Be - bop - a - lu - la, she's my ba - by. Be - bop - a - lu - la, I don't mean may - be.

Be - bop - a - lu - la, she's my ba - by doll, my ba - by doll, my ba - by doll.

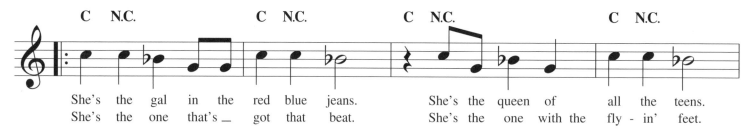

She's the gal in the red blue jeans. She's the queen of all the teens.
She's the one that's __ got that beat. She's the one with the fly - in' feet.

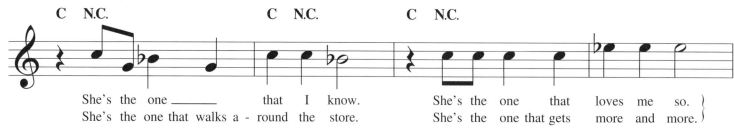

She's the one _____ that I know. She's the one that loves me so.
She's the one that walks a - round the store. She's the one that gets more and more.

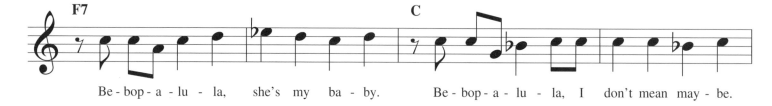

Be - bop - a - lu - la, she's my ba - by. Be - bop - a - lu - la, I don't mean may - be.

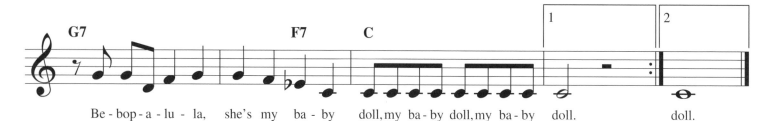

Be - bop - a - lu - la, she's my ba - by doll, my ba - by doll, my ba - by doll. doll.

BLUE EYES CRYING IN THE RAIN

Words and Music by
FRED ROSE

BELIEVE WHAT YOU SAY

Words and Music by DORSEY BURNETTE
and JOHNNY BURNETTE

I be - lieve what you say when you say you're go - in' stead - y with
lieve what you say when you say you don't miss

no - bod - y else but me.
no - bod - y else but me.
I be - lieve what you say when you say ya don't kiss

no - bod - y else but me. I be - lieve, do be - lieve, _____ I be - lieve, yeah, be -

lieve, pret - ty ba - by, be - lieve you're go - in' stead - y with no - bod - y else but me.

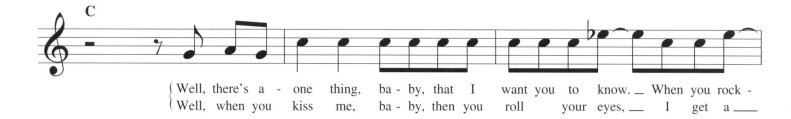

Well, there's a - one thing, ba - by, that I want you to know. _ When you rock -
Well, when you kiss me, ba - by, then you roll your eyes, _ I get a _

- in' with me, you don't a - rock too slow.   A - move on in, get   toe   to   toe. ___ We're gon - na
___ fun - ny feel - in' that I'm hyp - no - tized.   The chills run all up and down my spine _____ a-

rock   'til we can't _____   rock   no   more. ⎤ I   be - lieve,   do   be - lieve, _
tell - in' ev - 'ry - bod - y   that you're mine   all   mine. ⎦ I   be - lieve,   do   be - lieve, _

_____   I   be - lieve,   yeah, be - lieve, pret - ty ba - by,   be - lieve you're go - in' stead - y with

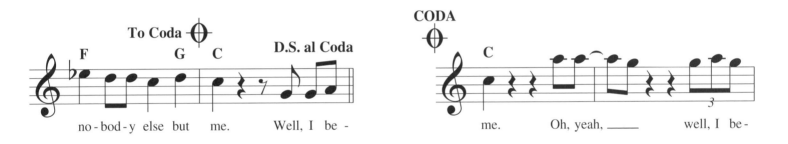

no - bod - y else but   me.   Well, I be -   me.   Oh, yeah, _____   well, I be -

lieve,   do be - lieve, _____   I be - lieve,   well, be - lieve, pret - ty ba - by,   be-

lieve you're go - in' stead - y with   no - bod - y else but   me.

BLACK DENIM TROUSERS AND MOTORCYCLE BOOTS

Words and Music by JERRY LEIBER
and MIKE STOLLER

Briskly

He wore black den-im trou-sers and mo-tor-cy-cle boots and a

black leath-er jack-et with an ea-gle on the back. He

had a hopped-up cy-cle that took off like a gun. That

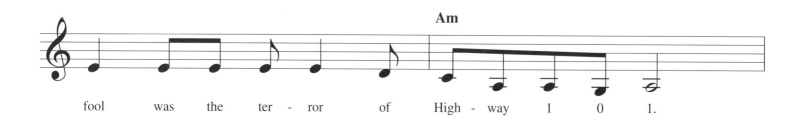

fool was the ter-ror of High-way 1 0 1.

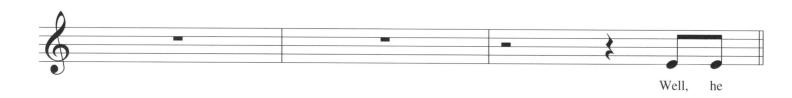

Well, he

nev-er washed his face and he nev-er combed his hair. He had
Lou, poor girl, she plead-ed and she begged him not to leave. She

ax - le grease em - bed - ded un - der - neath his fin - ger - nails. On the
said, "I've got a feel - ing if you ride to - night I'll grieve." But her

mus - cle of his arm was a red tat - too, a pic - ture of a heart say - ing,
tears were shed in vain, and her ev -'ry word was lost in the rum - ble of his en - gine and the

"Moth - er, I _____ love you." He had a pret - ty girl - friend by the
smoke from his ex - haust. He took off like a dev - il, there was

name of Mar - y Lou, but he treat - ed her just like he
fi - re in his eyes. He said, "I'll go a thou - sand miles be -

treat - ed all _____ the rest. And ev -'ry - bod - y pit - ied her ___ 'cause
fore the sun can rise." But he hit a scream - ing die - sel that was

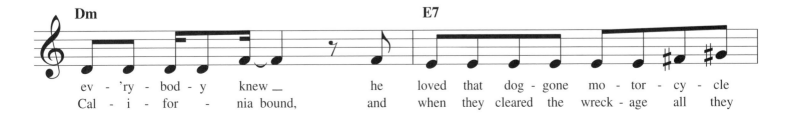

ev -'ry - bod - y knew _ he loved that dog - gone mo - tor - cy - cle
Cal - i - for - nia bound, and when they cleared the wreck - age all they

best. He wore black den-im trou-sers and mo-tor-cy-cle boots and a
found was his

black leath-er jack-et with an ea-gle on the back. He
But they

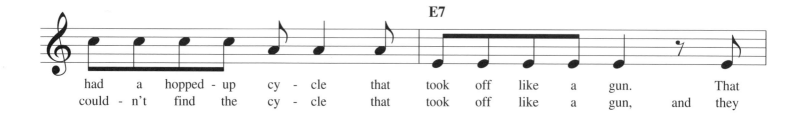

had a hopped-up cy-cle that took off like a gun. That
could-n't find the cy-cle that took off like a gun, and they

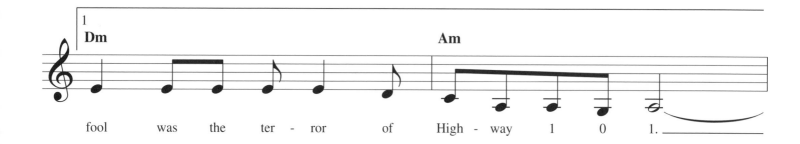

fool was the ter-ror of High-way 1 0 1.

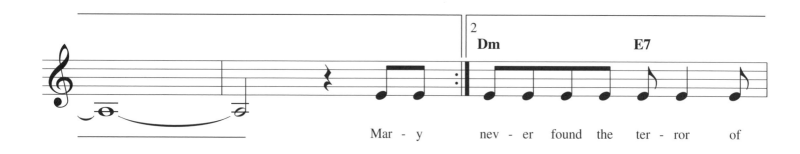

Mar-y nev-er found the ter-ror of

High-way 1 0 1.

BLUE SUEDE SHOES

Words and Music by
CARL LEE PERKINS

BOOT SCOOTIN' BOOGIE

Words and Music by
RONNIE DUNN

Moderate Shuffle

Out in the coun-try past the cit-y lim-it sign, __ well, there's a hon-ky-tonk __ near the
got a good job, I work hard for my mon-ey. When it's quit-tin' time, __ I
Instrumental solo
bar-ten-der asks me, says, "Son, what will it be?" __ I want a shot at that red-head yon-der

coun-ty line. __ The joint starts jump-in' ev-'ry night when the sun __ goes
hit the door run-nin'. I fire up my pick-up and let the hors-es
(Solo)
look-in' at me. __ The dance floor's hop-pin' and it's hot-ter than the Fourth of Ju-

down. __ They got whis-key, wom-en, __
run. __ I go fly-in' down that high-way
(Solo)
ly. __ I see out-laws, in-laws, __

mu-sic and smoke. __ It's where all the cow-boy folk __ go to boot scoot-in'
to that hide-a-way __ stuck out in the woods, to do the boot scoot-in'
(Solo)
crooks __ and straights __ all out __ mak-in' it shake do-in' the boot scoot-in'

1, 3

2, 4

boo - gie. __ I've
boo - gie. __ Yeah, __
(Solo)   *Solo ends*   The
boo - gie. __ Yeah, __

heel to toe, do-cie-doe, come on, ba-by, let's go boot scoot-in'!

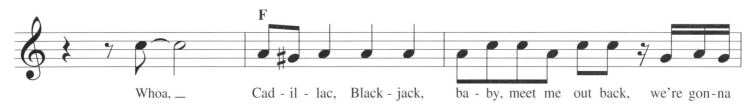

Whoa, — Cad - il - lac, Black - jack, ba - by, meet me out back, we're gon-na

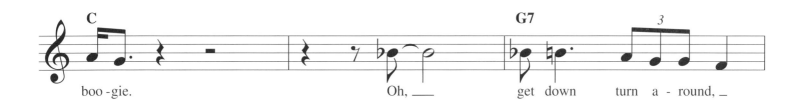

boo -gie. Oh, ___ get down turn a - round, —

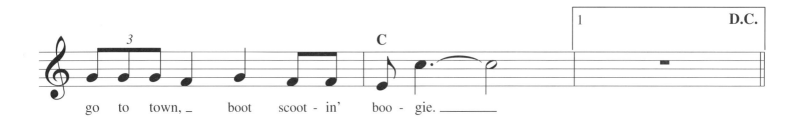

go to town, — boot scoot - in' boo - gie. ___

Whoa, — I ___ said, get down, turn a - round, —

go to town, — boot scoot - in' boo - gie. ___ Whoa, —

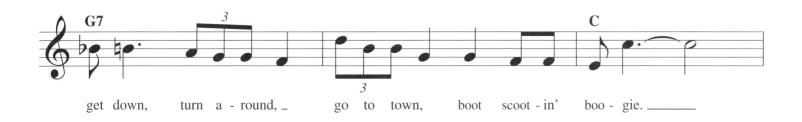

get down, turn a - round, — go to town, boot scoot - in' boo - gie. ___

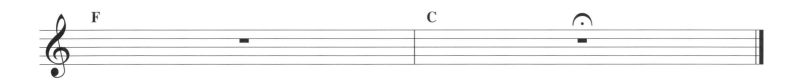

BRAND NEW MAN

Words and Music by DON COOK,
RONNIE DUNN and KIX BROOKS

Moderate Country

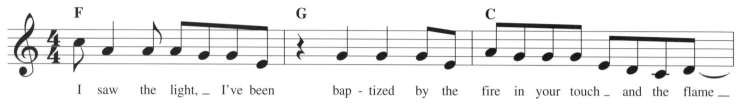

I saw the light, __ I've been bap - tized by the fire in your touch __ and the flame __

__ in your eyes. __ I'm born __ to love __ a - gain, _____ I'm a brand - new __

man. __

Well, the whole town's talk - in' 'bout the line _____ I'm walk - in' that
love 'em and leave 'em oh. __ I'd brag a - bout my free - dom, how

leads right to _____ your door. _____ Oh, how I used to __ roam, _____
no one could tie me down. _____ Then I met __ you, _____

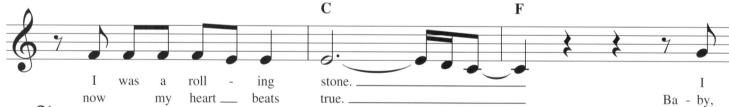

I was a roll - ing stone. _____ I
now my heart __ beats true. _____ Ba - by,

used to have a wild __ side, they say a coun - try mile __ wide. I'd burn those _ beer _ joints _ down. __
you and me to - geth - er feels more __ like _ for - ev - er than an - y - thing _ I've _ ev - er known. _

(D.S.) *Instrumental solo*

__ That's all __ changed now, _____ you turned my life __ a - round. __
__ We're right on track, _____ I ain't a - look - in' back. __

33

BREAD AND BUTTER

Words and Music by LARRY PARKS
and JAY TURNBOW

Moderate Rock

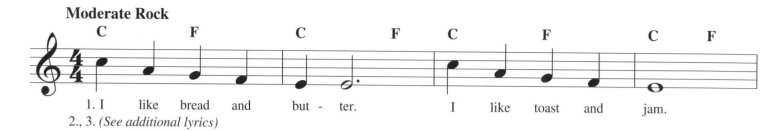

1. I like bread and but-ter. I like toast and jam.
2., 3. *(See additional lyrics)*

That's what my ba-by feeds ___ me. I'm her lov-in' man.

He likes bread and but-ter. He likes toast and jam.

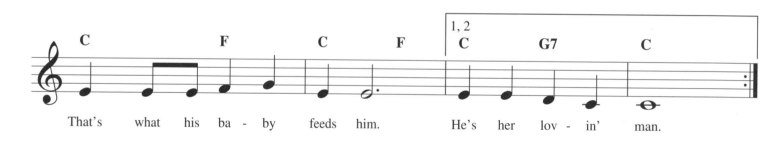

That's what his ba-by feeds him. He's her lov-in' man.

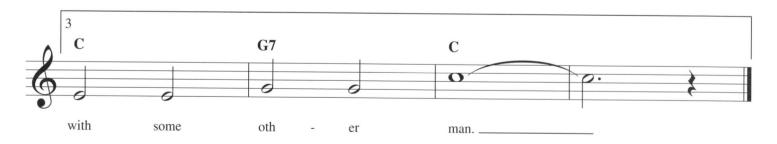

with some oth-er man. ___

Additional Lyrics

2. She don't cook mashed potatoes,
   Don't cook T-bone steak.
   Don't feed me peanut butter.
   She knows that I can't take
   No more bread and butter,
   No more toast and jam.
   He found his baby eatin'
   With some other man.

3. Got home early one mornin'
   Much to my surprise,
   She was eatin' chicken and dumplin's
   With some other guy.
   No more bread and butter,
   No more toast and jam.
   I found my baby eatin'
   With some other man.

CHANTILLY LACE

Words and Music by
J.P. RICHARDSON

Moderate Boogie Woogie

Chan - til - ly lace _____ and a pret - ty face _____

_____ and a po - ny - tail _____ hang - in' down, _____

_____ wig - gle in her walk and a gig - gle in her

talk, makes the world go 'round. _____ Ain't

noth - in' in this world like a big - eyed girl _____ to make me

act so fun - ny, make me spend my mon - ey, make me

feel real loose like a long - necked goose, like a girl. _____

BYE BYE LOVE

Words and Music by FELICE BRYANT
and BOUDLEAUX BRYANT

Medium Swing

There goes my ba - by _____ with some - one new.

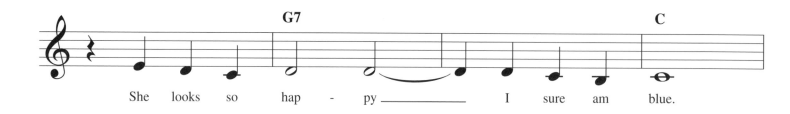

She looks so hap - py _____ I sure am blue.

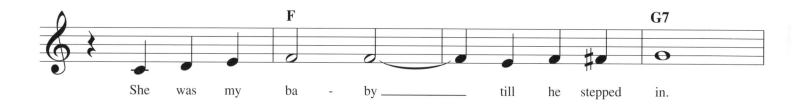

She was my ba - by _____ till he stepped in.

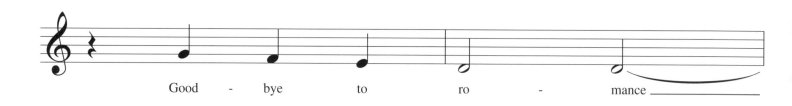

Good - bye to ro - mance _____

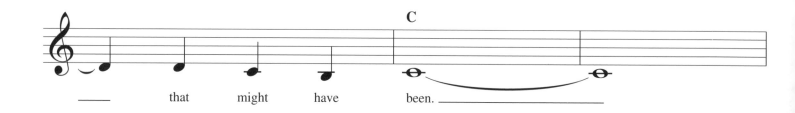

_____ that might have been. _____

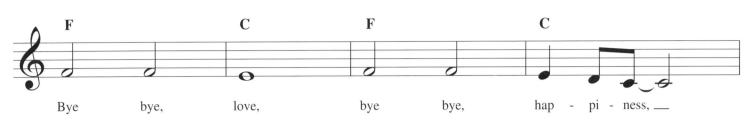

Bye   bye,   love,   bye   bye,   hap - pi - ness, __

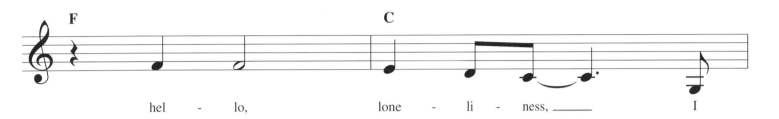

hel - lo,   lone - li - ness, _____   I

think   I'm   gon - na   cry. _____

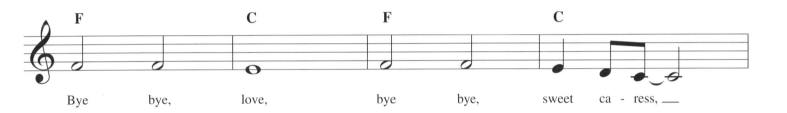

Bye   bye,   love,   bye   bye,   sweet   ca - ress, __

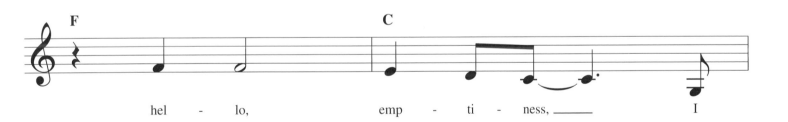

hel - lo,   emp - ti - ness, _____   I

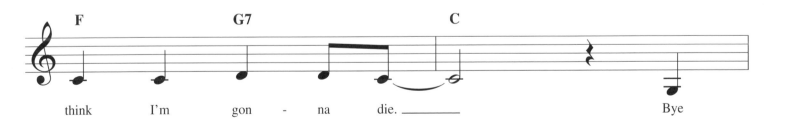

think   I'm   gon - na   die. _____   Bye

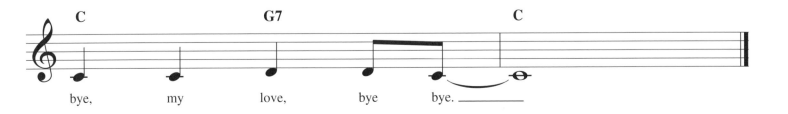

bye,   my   love,   bye   bye. _____

CHERRY, CHERRY

Words and Music by
NEIL DIAMOND

Brightly

Ba - by loves ___ me, yes, yes, ___ she does.
Y'ain't got no ___ right, no, no, ___ you don't,
Ah, the
ah, to

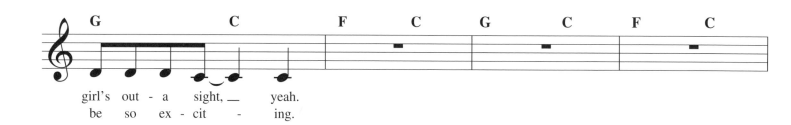

girl's out - a sight, ___ yeah.
be so ex - cit - ing.

Says she loves ___ me, yes, yes, ___ she does.
Won't need bright ___ lights, no, no, ___ we won't.
Gon - na
Gon - na

show me to - night, ___ yeah.)
make our own light - ning.)
She got the way to move ___ me, Cher - ry.

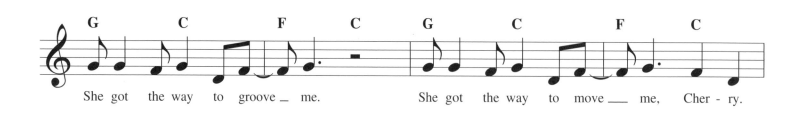

She got the way to groove ___ me.
She got the way to move ___ me, Cher - ry.

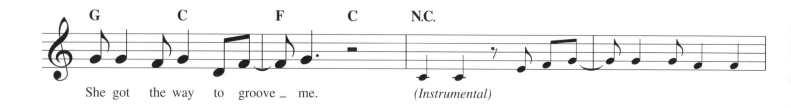

She got the way to groove ___ me.
(Instrumental)

CLOSER TO FREE

Words and Music by SAM LLANAS
and KURT NEUMANN

Fast, driving Rock

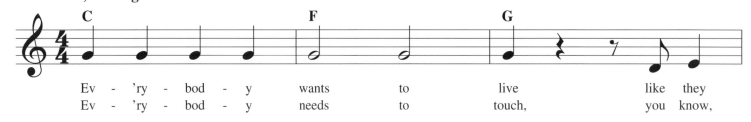

Ev - 'ry - bod - y wants to live like they
Ev - 'ry - bod - y needs to touch, you know,

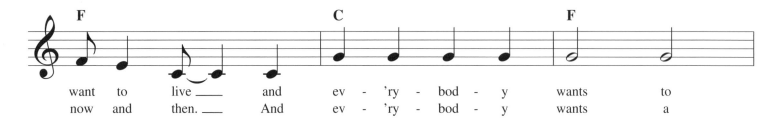

want to live ____ and ev - 'ry - bod - y wants to
now and then. ____ And ev - 'ry - bod - y wants a

love like they want to love. ____ Ev - 'ry - bod - y
good, good friend. Ev - 'ry - bod - y

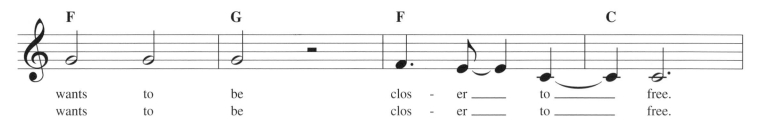

wants to be clos - er ____ to _____ free.
wants to be clos - er ____ to _____ free.

To Coda

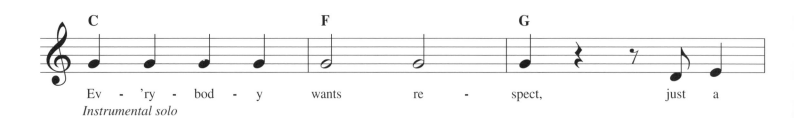

Ev - 'ry - bod - y wants re - spect, just a
Instrumental solo

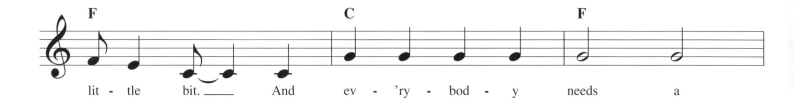

lit - tle bit. ____ And ev - 'ry - bod - y needs a

COAT OF MANY COLORS

Words and Music by
DOLLY PARTON

Moderately

Back through the years I go wan - d'ring once a - gain, back to the sea - sons of my youth. I re-call a box of rags that some - one gave us and how my ma - ma put the rags to use. There were

rags of man - y col - ors but ev - 'ry piece was small, and I
sewed, she told a sto - ry from the Bi - ble she had read, a - bout a
patch - es on my britch - es and holes in both my shoes, in my
could - n't un - der - stand it, for I felt I was rich, and I

did - n't have a coat and it was way down in the fall. Ma - ma
coat of man - y col - ors Jo - seph wore. And then she said, "Per-
coat of man - y col - ors I hur - ried off to school just to
told 'em of the love my ma - ma sewed in ev - 'ry stitch. And I

sewed the rags to - geth - er, sew - ing ev - 'ry piece with love. She made my
haps this coat will bring you good luck and hap - pi - ness." And I just
find the oth - ers laugh - ing and a - mak - ing fun of me in my
told them all the sto - ry Ma - ma told me while she sewed and how my

DA DOO RON RON
(When He Walked Me Home)

Words and Music by ELLIE GREENWICH,
JEFF BARRY and PHIL SPECTOR

DADDY SANG BASS

Words and Music by
CARL PERKINS

DON'T WORRY, BE HAPPY

Words and Music by
BOBBY McFERRIN

Whistle

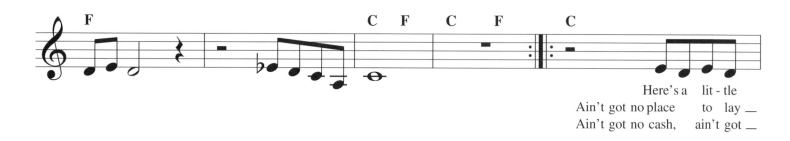

Here's a   lit - tle
Ain't got no place   to lay —
Ain't got no cash,   ain't got —

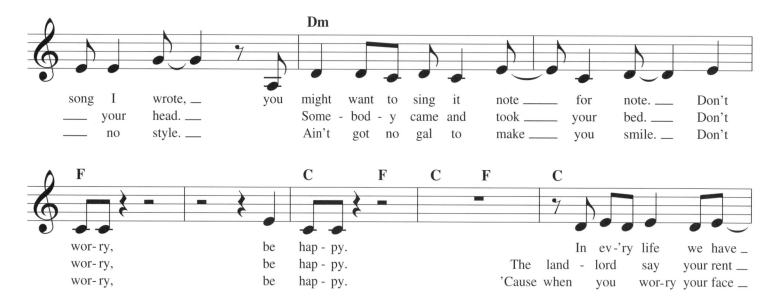

song   I   wrote, —   you   might   want   to   sing   it   note _____   for   note. _____   Don't
_____   your   head. _____   Some - bod - y   came   and   took _____   your   bed. _____   Don't
_____   no   style. _____   Ain't   got   no   gal   to   make _____   you   smile. _____   Don't

wor - ry,   be   hap - py.   In   ev - 'ry   life   we   have _
wor - ry,   be   hap - py.   The   land - lord   say   your   rent _
wor - ry,   be   hap - py.   'Cause   when   you   wor - ry   your   face _

_____   some   trou - ble,   but   when   you   wor - ry   you   make _____   it   dou - ble. Don't
_____   is   late, _____   he   may   have   to   lit - i - gate.   Don't
_____   will   frown, _____   and   that   will   bring   ev - 'ry - bod - y   down.   Don't

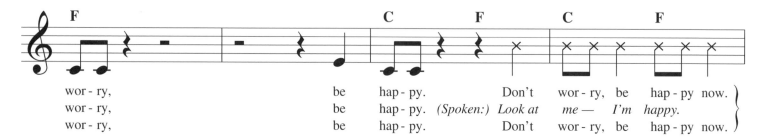

wor - ry,   be   hap - py.   Don't   wor - ry,   be   hap - py   now.
wor - ry,   be   hap - py. (Spoken:) Look at   me — I'm   happy.
wor - ry,   be   hap - py.   Don't   wor - ry,   be   hap - py   now.

DONNA

Words and Music by
RITCHIE VALENS

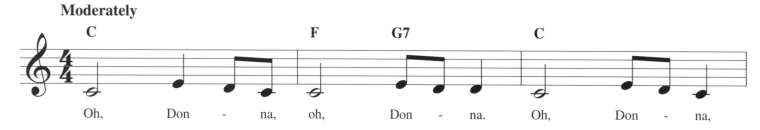

Oh, Don - na, oh, Don - na. Oh, Don - na,

oh, Don - na. I had a girl, ___ Don - na was her name.
Now that you're gone, ___ I'm left all a - lone,

Since she left me ___ I've nev - er been the same, }
all by my - self ___ to wan - der and ___ roam, } 'cause I

love my ___ girl. ___ Don - na, ___ where can you be, ___

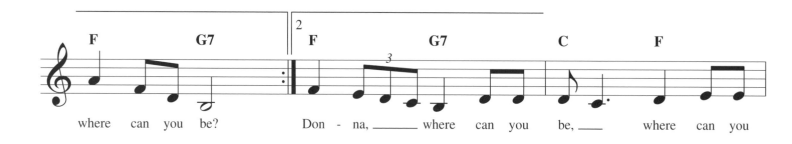

where can you be? Don - na, ___ where can you be, ___ where can you

be? ___ Oh, dar - lin,' ___ now that you're gone, I don't

know   what   I'll   do.   All _____ my   smiles   and all   my

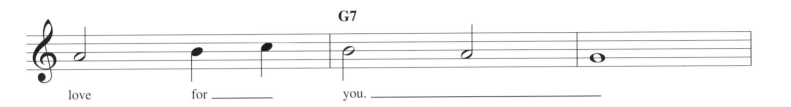

love   for _____   you. _____

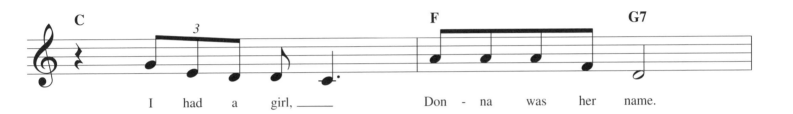

I   had   a   girl, _____   Don - na   was   her   name.

Since   she   left   me _____   I've   nev - er   been   the   same,   'cause   I

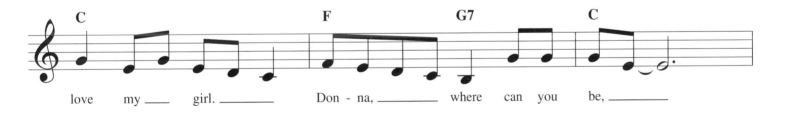

love   my ___   girl. _____   Don - na, _____   where   can   you   be, _____

where   can   you   be?   Oh,   Don - na,   oh,   Don - na.

Oh,   Don - na,   oh,   Don - na.   oh.

DREAMS

Words and Music by
STEVIE NICKS

Moderately, with a beat

ELVIRA

Words and Music by
DALLAS FRAZIER

Moderate Country beat

El - vi - ra, El - vi - ra,

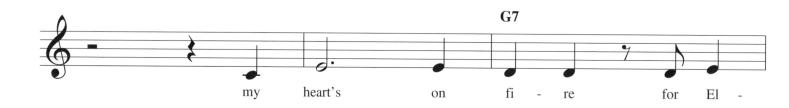

my heart's on fi - re for El -

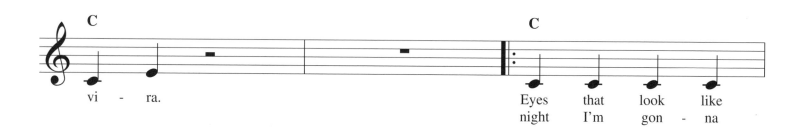

vi - ra. Eyes that look like
night I'm gon - na

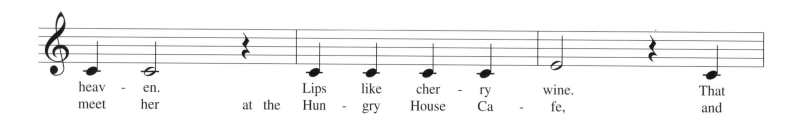

heav - en. Lips like cher - ry wine. That
meet her at the Hun - gry House Ca - fe, and

girl can sho' nuff make my lit - tle light shine. _____
I'm gon-na give her all the love I can. _____

_____ I get a fun - ny feel - ing
She's gon - na jump and hol - ler, 'cause I

EVIL WAYS

Words and Music by
SONNY HENRY

Moderate Latin

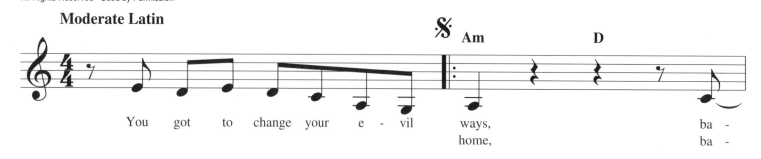

You got to change your e - vil ways, ba-
home, ba-

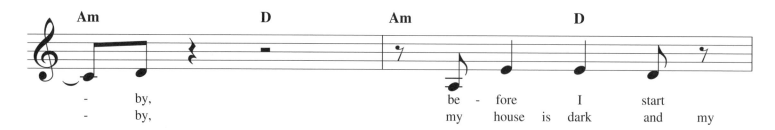

- by, be - fore I start
- by, my house is dark and my

lov - in' you. You got to change,___ ba-
thoughts are cold. You hang a - round,___ ba-

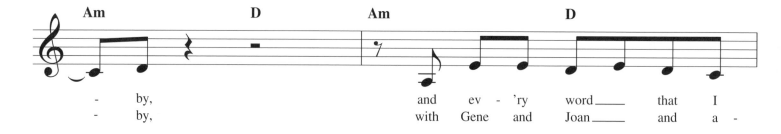

- by, and ev - 'ry word___ that I
- by, with Gene and Joan___ and a-

say is true. You got me run - nin' and hid - in' all___
who knows who. I'm get - tin' tired___ of wait - in' and

___ o - ver town.___ You got me sneak - in' and a - peep - in' and
fool - in' a - round.___ I'll find some - bod - y that___ won't make me

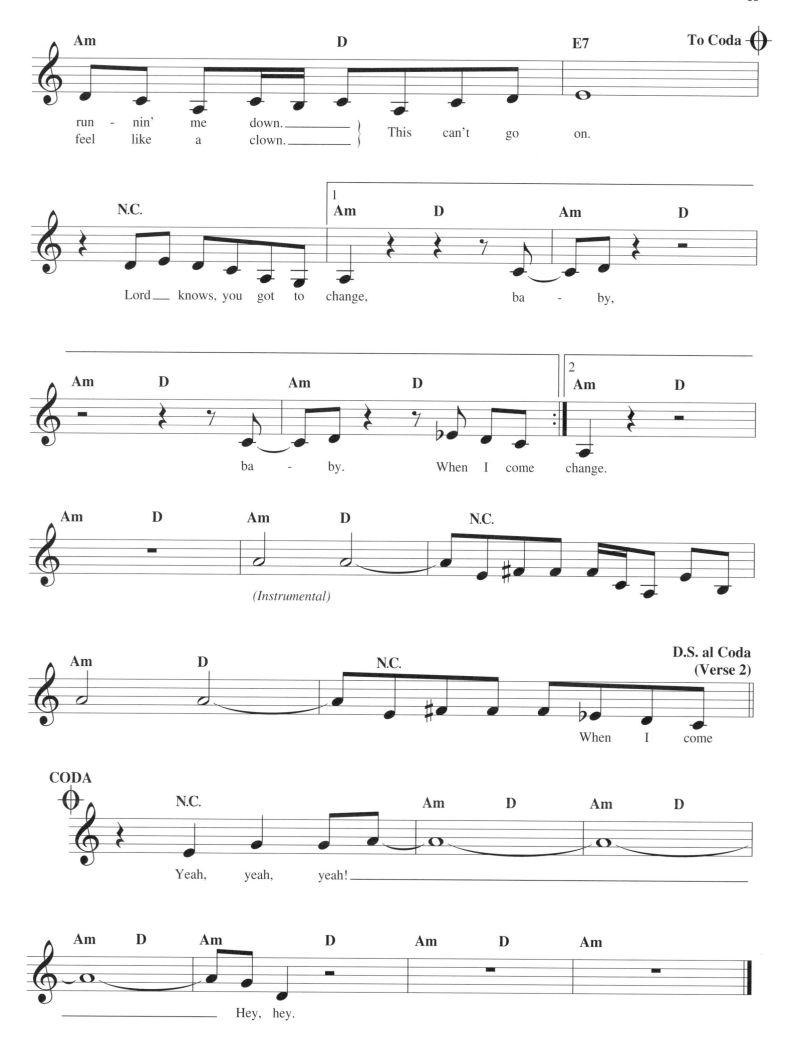

THE FIRST CUT IS THE DEEPEST

Words and Music by
CAT STEVENS

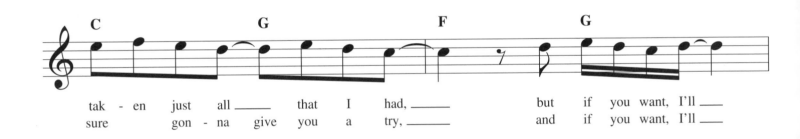

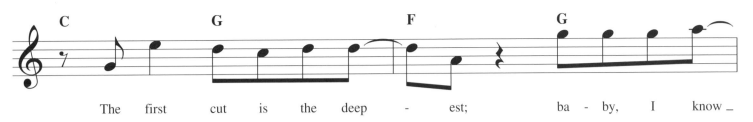

The first cut is the deep - est; ba - by, I know _

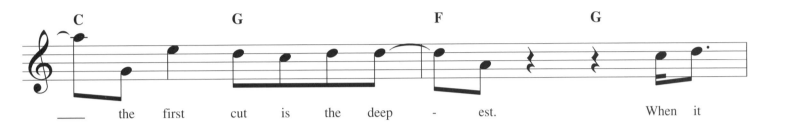

_ the first cut is the deep - est. When it

comes to be - in' luck - y she's cursed. _____ When it

comes to lov - in' me she's worse. _ I still

comes to lov - in' me she's worse. _____

FLY LIKE AN EAGLE

Words and Music by
STEVE MILLER

Moderately, in 2

Tip   top ___ tip.   Doot   doot   doo   doo.

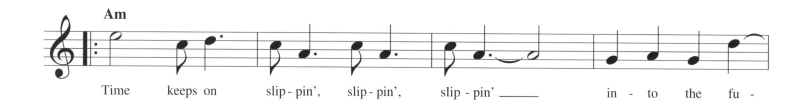

Time   keeps   on   slip - pin',   slip - pin',   slip - pin' ____   in - to   the   fu -

- ture. ____

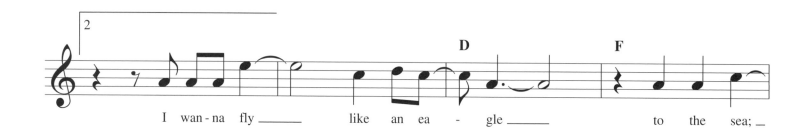

I   wan - na   fly ____   like   an   ea - gle ____   to   the   sea; ___

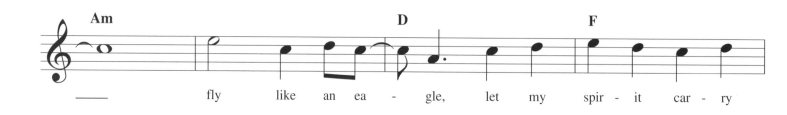

___   fly   like   an   ea - gle,   let   my   spir - it   car - ry

me.   I   want   to   fly   like   an   ea - gle ____   till   I'm   free, _

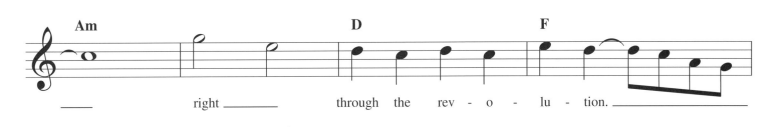

right _____ through the rev - o - lu - tion. _____

_____ Feed the ba - bies who don't have e - nough _ to eat.

Shoe the chil - dren with no shoes on ____ their feet.

House the peo - ple liv - in' in ____ the street.

Oh, _____ there's a so - lu - tion.

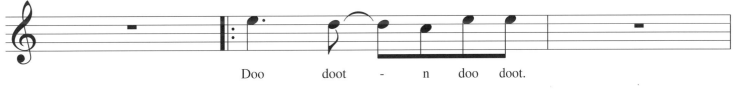

Doo doot - n doo doot.

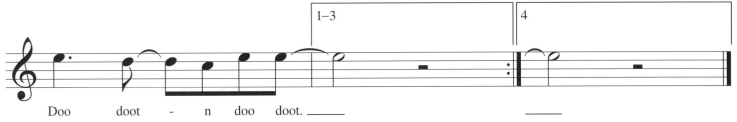

Doo doot - n doo doot. _____ _____

THE GAMBLER

Words and Music by
DON SCHLITZ

Moderately Country, in 2

On a warm sum-mer's eve - nin' on a train bound for no - where, I

met up with The Gam - bler; we were both too tired to sleep. ___ So

we took turns ___ a - star - in' out the win - dow at the dark - ness 'til

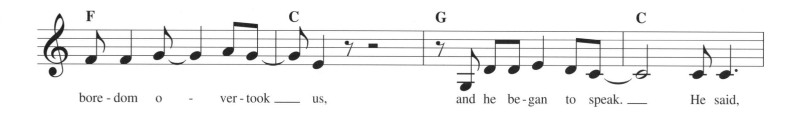

bore - dom o - ver - took ___ us, and he be - gan to speak. ___ He said,

"Son, I've made a life ___ out of read - in' peo - ple's fac - es, and

know - in' what their cards ___ were by the way they held ___ their eyes. ___ And if

you don't mind ___ my say - in', I can see you're out ___ of ac - es. For a

61

taste of your whis - key I'll give you some ad - vice." ___

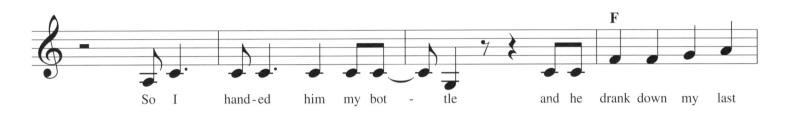

So I hand-ed him my bot - tle and he drank down my last

swal - low. Then he bummed a cig - a - rette ___ and asked me for a light. ___

___ And the night got death - ly qui - et, and his face lost all ex - pres -

- sion. Said, if you're gon - na play ___ the game, ___ boy, ya got-ta learn to play ___ it right. ___

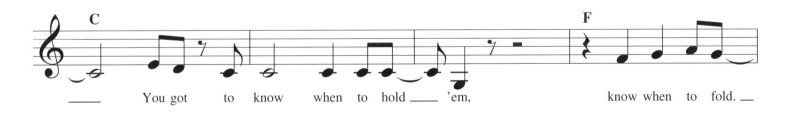

___ You got to know when to hold ___ 'em, know when to fold. ___

___ 'em, know when to walk ___ a - way ___ and know when to run. ___

62

You nev-er count your mon-ey when you're sit-tin' at the ta - ble. There'll be

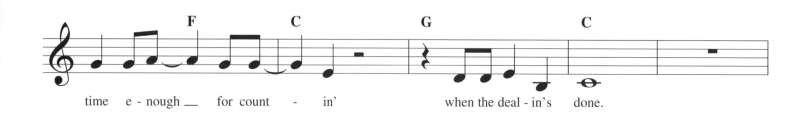

time e-nough __ for count - in' when the deal-in's done.

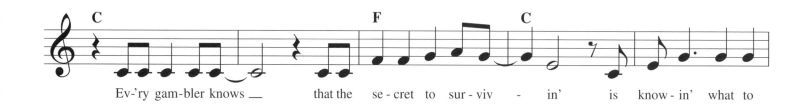

Ev-'ry gam-bler knows __ that the se-cret to sur-viv - in' is know-in' what to

throw a-way __ and know-in' what to keep. __ 'Cause ev-'ry hand's a win - ner and

ev-'ry hand's a los - er, and the best that you __ can hope for is to

die in your sleep." And when he'd fin-ished speak - in', he

turned back towards the win - dow, crushed out his cig-a-rette __ and

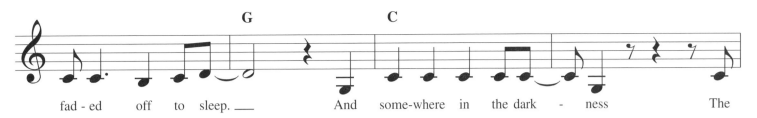

fad - ed   off   to   sleep. ___   And   some-where in   the dark - ness   The

Gam - bler,   he   broke   e - ven.   But   in   his   fi - nal words ___   I   found   an

ace   that I ___ could keep. ___   You got   to   know when to hold ___ 'em,

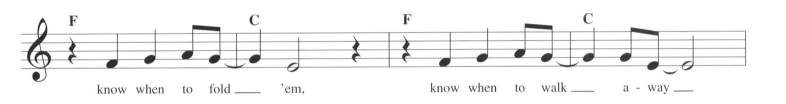

know when to fold ___ 'em,   know when to walk ___ a - way ___

and know when to run. ___   You nev - er count   your   mon - ey   when you're

sit - tin'   at   the   ta - ble. There'll be time e - nough ___ for count - in'

when the deal - in's done.   You got   to   done.

GET BACK

Words and Music by JOHN LENNON
and PAUL McCARTNEY

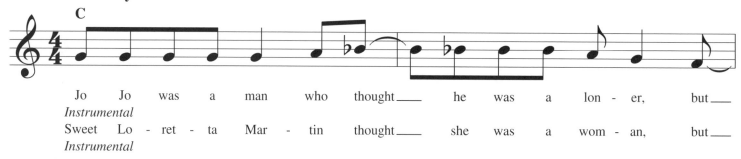

Jo Jo was a man who thought___ he was a lon - er, but___
Instrumental
Sweet Lo - ret - ta Mar - tin thought___ she was a wom - an, but___
Instrumental

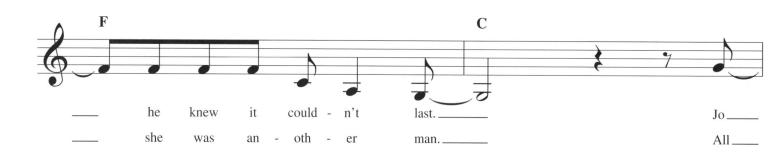

___ he knew it could - n't last._____ Jo
___ she was an - oth - er man._____ All

_____ Jo left his home in Tuc - son, Ar - i - zo - na for___
_____ the girls a - round her say_____ she's got it com - ing,

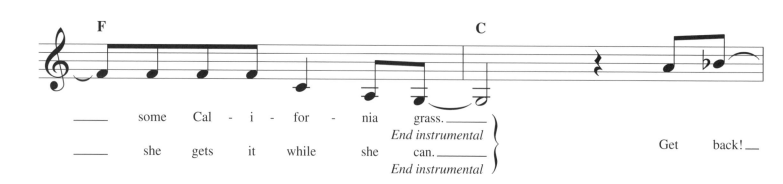

_____ some Cal - i - for - nia grass._____
End instrumental
_____ she gets it while she can._____
End instrumental

Get back!

___ Get back!_____   Get back___

to where you once be - longed._____ Get back!__

Get back!_____ Get back___

to where you once be - longed._____ (*Get back, Jo Jo*)

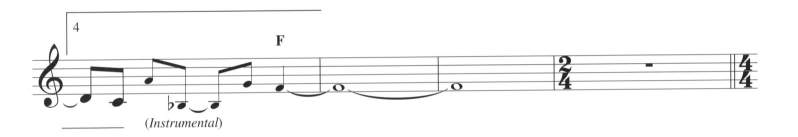

(*Instrumental*)

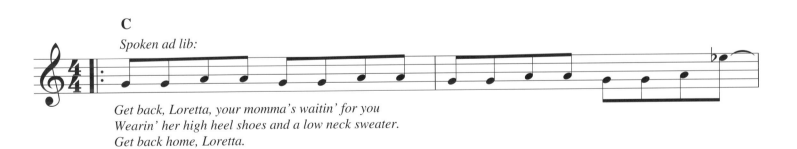

Spoken ad lib:

Get back, Loretta, your momma's waitin' for you
Wearin' her high heel shoes and a low neck sweater.
Get back home, Loretta.

Repeat and Fade

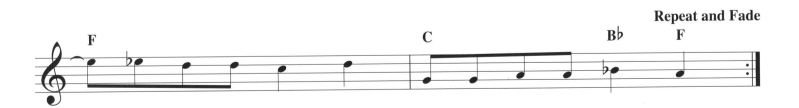

GOOD GOLLY MISS MOLLY

Words and Music by ROBERT BLACKWELL
and JOHN MARASCALCO

GIVE ME ONE REASON

Words and Music by
TRACY CHAPMAN

Medium Blues

Give me one rea - son to stay here and I'll turn right back a -

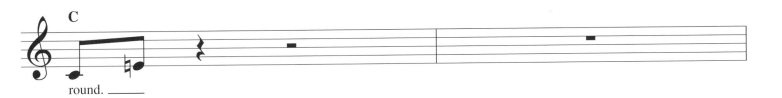

round. ____

Give me one rea - son to stay here ____ and I'll turn right back a -

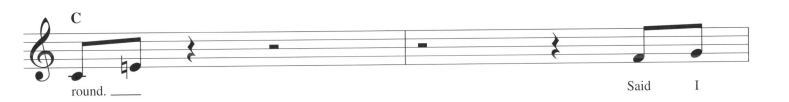

round. ____ Said I

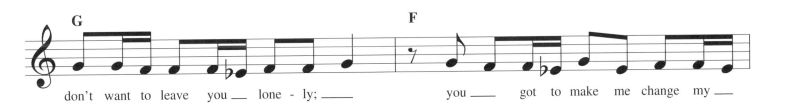

don't want to leave you ____ lone - ly; ____ you ____ got to make me change my ____

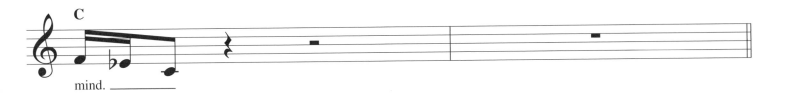

mind. ____

69

THE GREEN DOOR

Words and Music by BOB DAVIE
and MARVIN MOORE

Moderately

Mid - night ___ one more night with - out sleep - in'. ___
Knocked once ___ tried to tell 'em I'd been there. ___

___ Watch - ing ___ till the morn - ing comes
___ Door slammed ___ hos - pi - tal - i - ty's

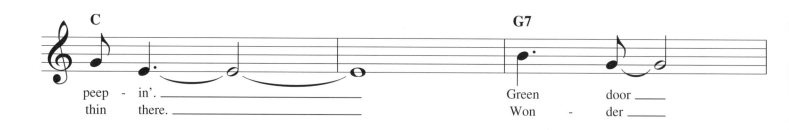

peep - in'. ___ Green door ___
thin there. ___ Won - der ___

what's the se - cret you're keep - in'. ___ There's an
just what's go - in' on in there. ___ Saw an

old pi - a - no and they play it hot _____ be - hind the
eye - ball peep - in' thru a smok - y cloud _____ be - hind the

green door. _____ Don't know what they're do - in' but they
green door. _____ When I said Joe sent _____ me some - one

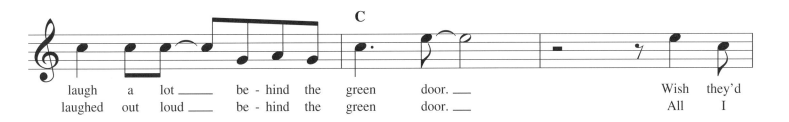

laugh a lot _____ be - hind the green door. _____ Wish they'd
laughed out loud _____ be - hind the green door. _____ All I

let me in _____ so I could find out what's _____ be - hind the
want to do _____ is join the hap - py crew _____ be - hind the

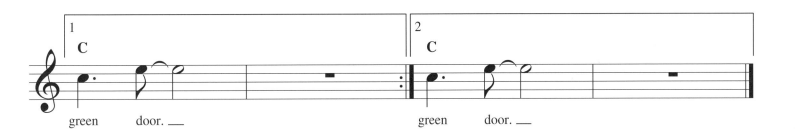

green door. _____

green door. _____

HANG ON SLOOPY

Words and Music by WES FARRELL
and BERT RUSSELL

Moderately

Hang on, Sloo - py, Sloo - py hang on.

Sloo - py lives ___ in a ver - y bad ___ part of town.
Sloo - py, I don't ___ care what your ___ dad - dy do.

All the girls I know ___ they try to put my Sloo - py down. ___
Don't you know, lit - tle girl, ___ I'm ___ in ___ love with you? ___

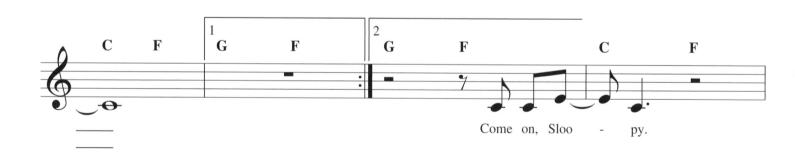

Come on, Sloo - py.

Come on, girl. ___ Say

yeah, yeah, yeah, ___ good, good, good, good,

good, good, good, good. ___ Oh, I wan - na say

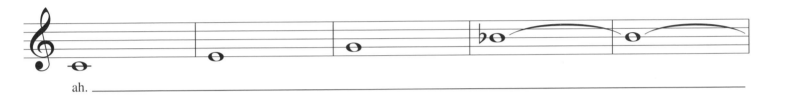

ah. ___

___ Now I want you to tell me some - thing, ba - by.

Well, don't it make you feel cra - zy? I wan - na say

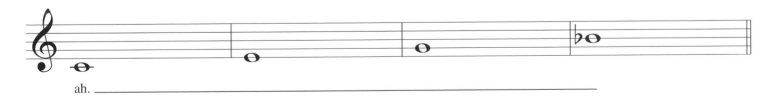

ah. ___

Repeat and Fade

Hang on, Sloo - py, Sloo - py hang on.

HANKY PANKY

Words and Music by JEFF BARRY
and ELLIE GREENWICH

Moderate Boogie-Rock

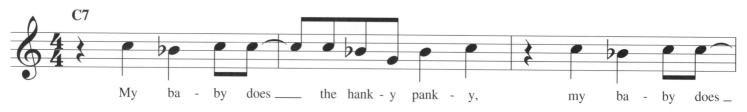

My ba - by does ___ the hank - y pank - y, my ba - by does ___

___ the hank - y pank - y, my ba - by does ___ the hank - y pank - y,

my ba - by does ___ the hank - y pank - y, my ba - by does ___

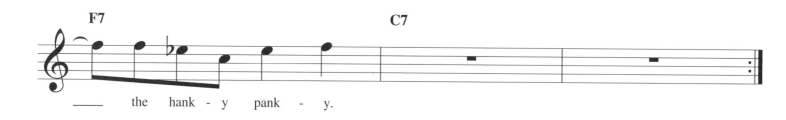

___ the hank - y pank - y.

I saw her walk - ing on down the line. ___ You know I saw her for the

ver - y first time, ___ a pret - ty lit - tle girl ___ stand - ing all a - lone. ___

Hey, pret - ty ba - by, can I take you home? __ I nev - er saw her, nev -

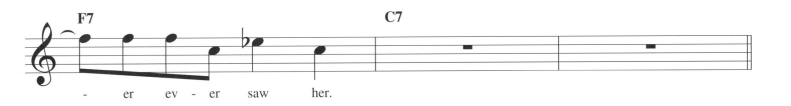

- er ev - er saw her.

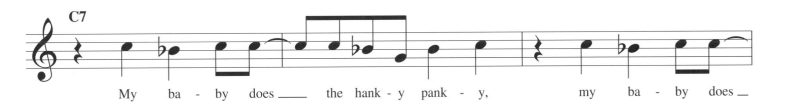

My ba - by does ___ the hank - y pank - y, my ba - by does ___

___ the hank - y pank - y, my ba - by does ___ the hank - y pank - y,

my ba - by does ___ the hank - y pank - y, my ba - by does ___

___ the hank - y pank - y.

HE STOPPED LOVING HER TODAY

Words and Music by BOBBY BRADDOCK
and CURLY PUTMAN

1. He said, "I'll love you 'til I die." She told him, "You'll for-get in time."
2. He kept some let-ters by his bed, dat-ed nine-teen six-ty-two.
3. *(See additional lyrics)*

As the years went slow-ly by, she still preyed up-on his mind.
He had un-der-lined in red ev-'ry sin-gle "I love you."

He kept her pic-ture on his wall and went half-cra-zy now and then.
I went to see him just to-day, oh, but I did-n't see no tears.

But he still loved her through it all, hop-ing she'd come back a-gain.
All dressed up to go a-way;

first time I'd seen him smile in years. He stopped lov-ing her to-day.

They placed a wreath up-on his door; and soon they'll car-ry him a-way.

He stopped lov-ing her to-day.

Additional Lyrics

3. *(Spoken:)* You know, she came to see him one last time.
   We all wondered if she would.
   And it came running through my mind,
   This time he's over her for good.
   Chorus

I FALL TO PIECES

Words and Music by HANK COCHRAN
and HARLAN HOWARD

Moderately

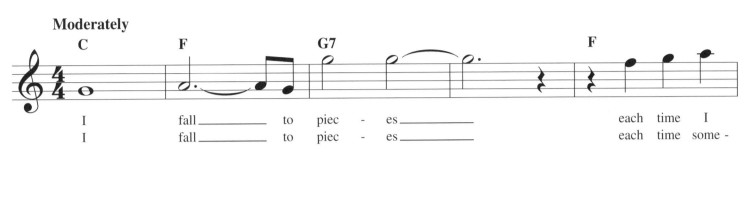

I fall to piec - es each time I
I fall to piec - es each time some -

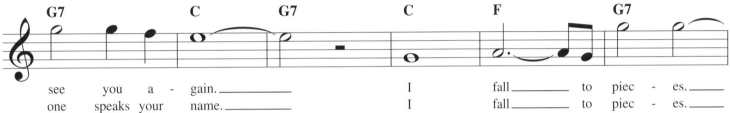

see you a - gain. I fall to piec - es.
one speaks your name. I fall to piec - es.

How can I be just your friend? You want me to
Time on - ly adds to the flame. You tell me to

act like we've nev - er kissed. You want me to for - get, pre - tend we've
find some - one else to love. Some - one who'll love me, too, the way you

nev - er met. And I've tried and I've tried, but I have - n't yet, } you walk
used to do. But each time I go out with some - one new, }

by and I fall to piec - es. piec - es.

HEARTBREAK HOTEL

Words and Music by MAE BOREN AXTON,
TOMMY DURDEN and ELVIS PRESLEY

Moderate Rock 'n' Roll

1. Now since my ba-by left me I've found a new place to dwell,
2.,3. *(See additional lyrics)*

down at the end ___ of Lone-ly Street at Heart-break Ho-tel, Well, I'm so

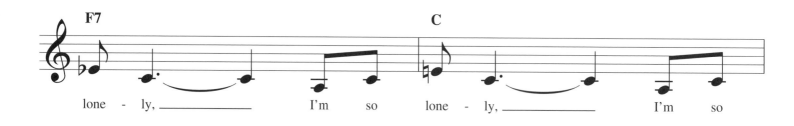

lone-ly, _____ I'm so lone-ly, _____ I'm so

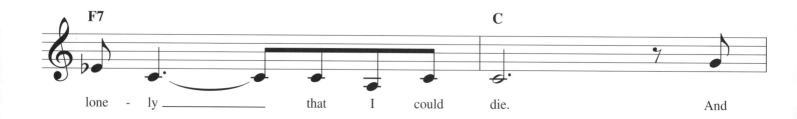

lone-ly _____ that I could die. And

tho' it's al - ways crowd - ed, you ___ can still find some room

for bro - ken - heart - ed lov - ers to cry there in ___ their gloom and be so

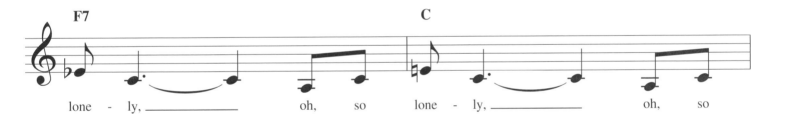

F7   **C**

lone - ly, ___ oh, so lone - ly, ___ oh, so

F7   1, 2 **C**   3 **C**

lone - ly, ___ they could die.   { 2. The / 3. So,   die.

Additional Lyrics

2. The bellhop's tears keep flowing,
   The desk clerk's dressed in black.
   They've been so long on Lonely Street,
   They'll never, they'll never look back.
   And they're so lonely, oh, they're so lonely,
   They're so lonely they pray to die.

3. So, if your baby leaves you
   And you have a tale to tell,
   Just take a walk down Lonely Street
   To Heartbreak Hotel, where you'll
   Be so lonely, you'll be so lonely,
   You'll be so lonely you could die.

HERE'S A QUARTER
(Call Someone Who Cares)

Words and Music by
TRAVIS TRITT

Rowdy Country Waltz

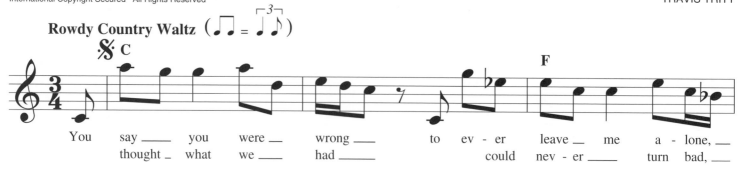

You say ___ you were ___ wrong ___ to ev - er leave ___ me a - lone, ___
thought ___ what we ___ had ___ could nev - er ___ turn bad, ___

___ and now you're sor - ry. You're lone - some ___ and scared. ___ And you
___ so your leav - ing caught me un - a - ware. ___ But the

say you'd be ___ hap - py if you could just ___ come back home. ___ Well, here's a
fact is you've ___ run. ___ Girl, ___ that can't ___ be un - done. ___ So here's a

quar - ter. ___ Call ___ some - one ___ who cares. ___
quar - ter. ___ Call ___ some - one ___ who cares. ___

Call

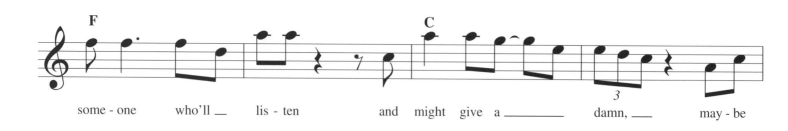

some - one who'll ___ lis - ten and might give a ___ damn, ___ may - be

one of ___ your ___ sor - did af - fairs. ___

But don't you

81

HOLD MY HAND

Words and Music by DARIUS CARLOS RUCKER,
EVERETT DEAN FELBER, MARK WILLIAM BRYAN
and JAMES GEORGE SONEFELD

Moderately

With a lit-tle love and some ten-der-ness __ we'll
day I saw you stand-ing there. _ Your
wast-ed and I was wast-ing time __ 'til

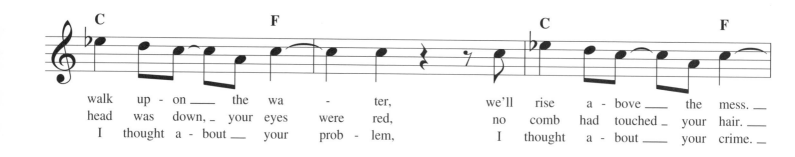

walk up-on __ the wa - ter, we'll rise a-bove __ the mess. __
head was down, _ your eyes were red, no comb had touched _ your hair. __
I thought a-bout __ your prob-lem, I thought a-bout __ your crime. __

__ With a lit-tle peace __ and some har-mo-ny __ we'll
__ I __ said, _ "Get _ up and let me see you smile. _ We'll
__ Then I stood _ up __ and I screamed a-loud, _ "Don't wan-na

take the world __ to-geth - er, we'll take 'em by __ the hand. __
take a walk __ to-geth - er, walk the road __ a while." __
be part of __ your prob - lem, don't wan-na be part of __ your crowd." __

__ 'Cause I got a hand for you. __
__ 'Cause I got a hand for you. __
__ 'Cause I got a hand for you. __ I got a hand for you. __
I got a hand for you. __

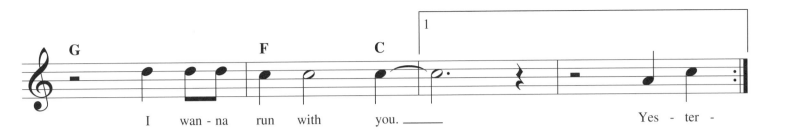

I wan - na run with you._____ Yes - ter -

____ (Won't you let me run ____ with you.) ____ Hold ____ my hand. ____

____ (Want you to hold my ____ hand.) Hold ____ my hand. ___

____ { I'll take you to a place ____ where you ____ can be ____
{ I'll take you to the prom - ised land. _____

an - y - thing you wan - na be ____ be - cause }
May - be we can't change ____ the world, but } I wan - na love you ____ the

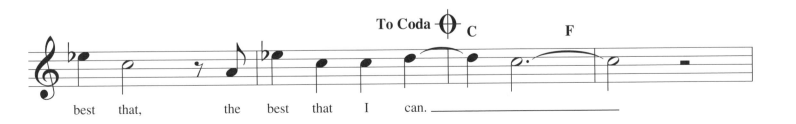

best that, the best that I can. _____

84

(Instrumental)

D.S. al Coda

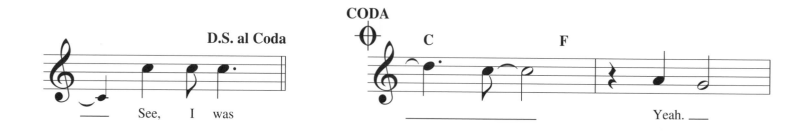

See,   I   was

CODA

_____   Yeah. ___

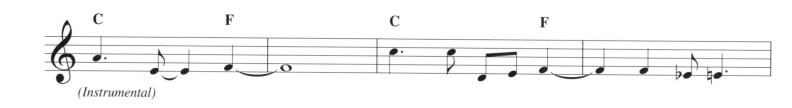

(Instrumental)

Hold _____   my   hand. ___

____ Want you   to   hold   my ___ hand. Hold _____   my   hand. ___

85

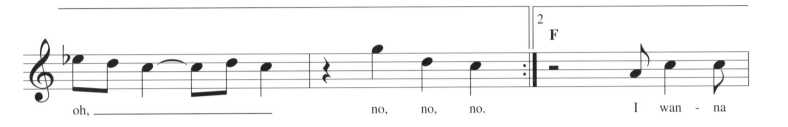

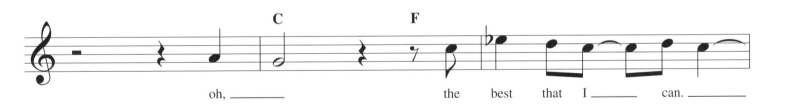

HONEY

Words and Music by
BOBBY RUSSELL

Moderately

1. See the tree, how big it's grown? But friend, it has-n't been too long, it
2. Then the first snow came and she ran out to brush the snow a-way so it

3.-8. *(See additional lyrics)*

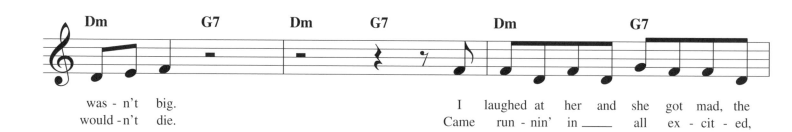

was-n't big.   I laughed at her and she got mad, the
would-n't die.   Came run-nin' in ____ all ex-cit-ed,

first day that she plant-ed it was just a twig.
slipped and al-most hurt her-self, I laughed 'til I cried.

1, 3, 5, 7

2, 4, 6, 8

Chorus

And Hon-ey, I miss you,

and I'm be-ing good. _____   And I'd love to be

with you ..... if on - ly I could.

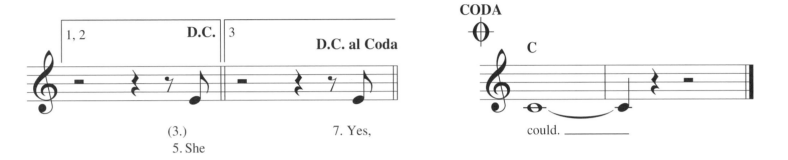

(3.)
5. She   7. Yes,   could. _____

Additional Lyrics

3. She was always young at heart,
   Kinda dumb and kinda smart and I loved her so.
   I surprised her with a puppy;
   Kept me up all Christmas Eve two years ago.

4. And it would sure embarrass her
   When I came home from working late 'cause I would know
   That she'd been sittin' there and cryin'
   Over some sad and silly late, late show.
   Chorus

5. She wrecked the car and she was sad
   And so afraid that I'd be mad, but what the heck.
   Tho' I pretended hard to be, guess you could say
   She saw through me and hugged my neck.

6. I came home unexpectedly and
   Found her crying needlessly in the middle of the day,
   And it was in the early Spring
   When flowers bloom and robins sing she went away.
   Chorus

7. Yes, one day while I wasn't home
   While she was there and all alone the angels came.
   Now all I have is memories of Honey,
   And I wake up nights and call her name.

8. Now my life's an empty stage
   Where Honey lived and Honey played and love grew up.
   A small cloud passes overhead and
   Cries down in the flower bed that Honey loved.
   Chorus

HONEYCOMB

Words and Music by
BOB MERRILL

Moderately

Hon - ey - comb, won't - cha be my ba - by? Hon - ey - comb, be my

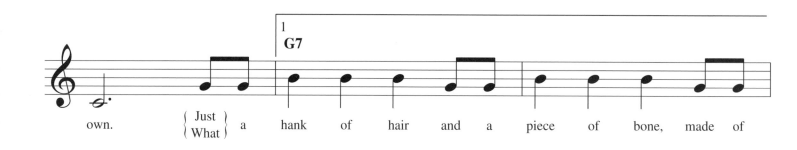

own. { Just / What } a hank of hair and a piece of bone, made of

walk - in' talk - in' Hon - ey - comb. ___ darn good life when I

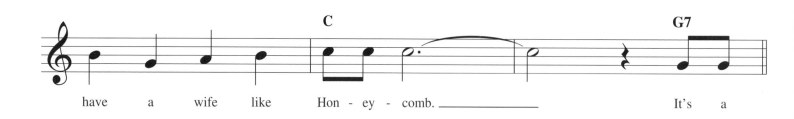

have a wife like Hon - ey - comb. _____ It's a

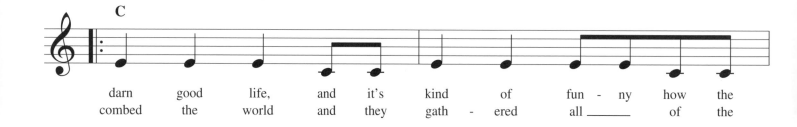

darn good life, and it's kind of fun - ny how the
combed the world and they gath - ered all _____ of the

89

bee was made and the bee made hon - ey. And the
hon - ey - comb in _____ one made sweet ball. _____ And the

hon - ey - bee, look - in' for a home,
hon - ey - comb from a mil - lion trips

made a hon - ey - comb. __ Then they   made   my

ba - by's lips. Hon - ey - comb, won't - cha be my ba - by?

Hon - ey - comb, be my own. What a darn good life when I

have a wife like Hon - ey - comb. _____

HOUND DOG

Words and Music by JERRY LEIBER
and MIKE STOLLER

You ain't noth-in' but a hound dog, ___ cry-in' all the

time. You ain't noth-in' but a hound dog, ___

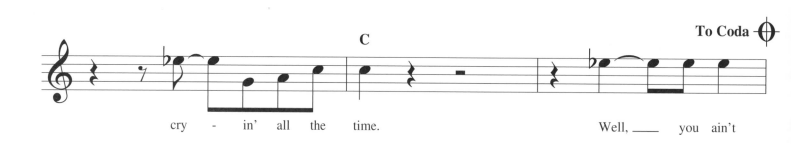

cry - in' all the time. Well, ___ you ain't

nev - er caught a rab - bit and you ain't no friend of mine. ___

Well, they said you was high - classed, _ but that was just a

lie.   Yeah, they said   you was   high - classed, __

but   that was just a   lie.   Yeah, ___   you ain't

nev - er caught a   rab - bit and you   ain't   no   friend   of   mine. ___

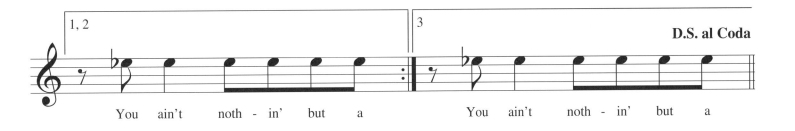

1, 2   You ain't   noth - in' but a   **3**   You ain't   noth - in' but a   **D.S. al Coda**

CODA

nev - er caught a   rab - bit, and you   ain't no   friend   of   mine. ___

I FEEL LUCKY

Words and Music by MARY CHAPIN CARPENTER
and DON SCHLITZ

To Coda ⊕

luck - y,   I feel ___ luck - y, _____ yeah. __

{ No ___ Pro - fes - sor Doom gon - na stand in my way. __ }
{ No trop - i - cal de - pres-sion gon - na steal my sun a - way. }

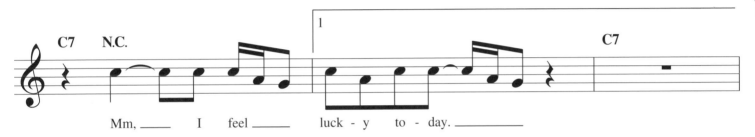

Mm, ___ I feel ___ luck - y to - day. _____

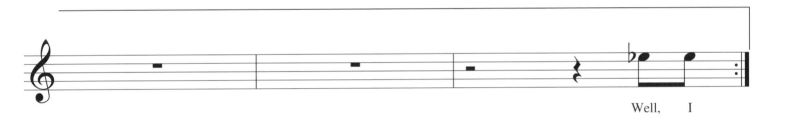

Well, I

luck - y to - day. _____   *(Instrumental)*

D.S. al Coda

Now e -

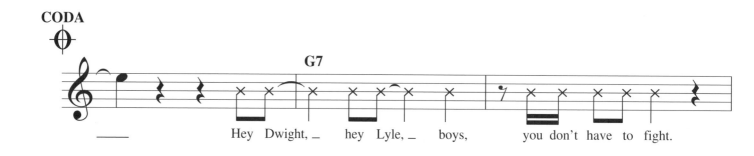

Hey Dwight, _ hey Lyle, _ boys, you don't have to fight.

Hot dog, _ I feel luck - y to - night. _ I feel _ luck - y,

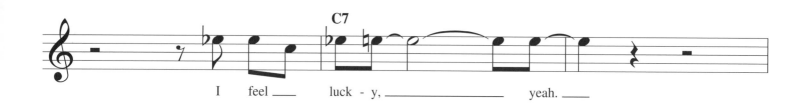

I feel _ luck - y, _____ yeah. ____

Think I'll flip a coin, I'm a win - ner ei - ther way. Mm, ___ I feel _____

luck - y to - day. _____

I FOUGHT THE LAW

Words and Music by
SONNY CURTIS

I GOT YOU
(I Feel Good)

Words and Music by
JAMES BROWN

Steady Rock/Funk

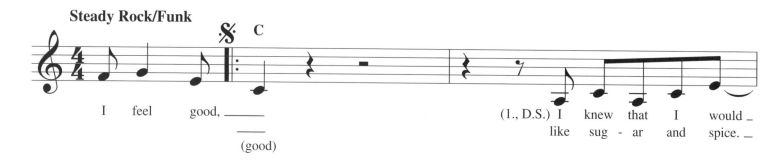

I feel good, _____
_____ (good)

(1., D.S.) I knew that I would _
like sug - ar and spice. _

_____ now.
_____

I feel good,
I feel nice,

F7

I knew that I would ___ now.
like sug - ar and spice. _____

C

To Coda ⊕

So good, _
So nice, _

_____ so good, _ }
_____ so nice, _ }

I got you. _____ (Instrumental)

G7   F7   1 C N.C.

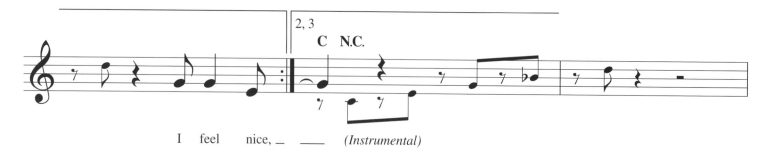

I feel nice, _ ___ (Instrumental)

2, 3 C N.C.

When I hold you in my arms, I

know that I can't do no wrong; _____ and when I hold ___ you in my

D.S. al Coda
(Verse 1)

arms, my love won't do you no harm. _____ And I feel

___ so good, ___ I got you. ___

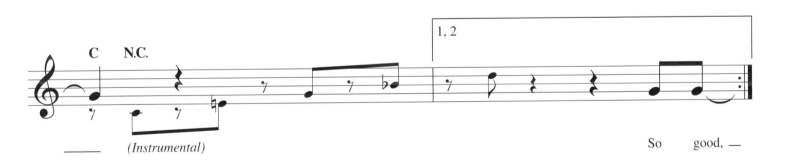

___ (Instrumental) So good, ___

Hey!

I LOVE ROCK 'N ROLL

Words and Music by ALAN MERRILL
and JAKE HOOKER

Moderately

I saw him danc - ing there ____ by the rec - ord ma -
smiled, so I got up ____ and asked ____ for his

chine.   I knew he must have been _
name.   "That don't mat - ter," he

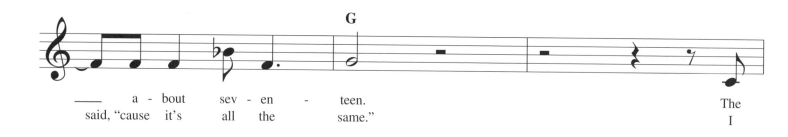

____ a - bout sev - en - teen.   The
said, "cause it's all the same."   I

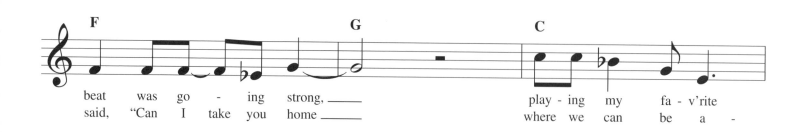

beat was go - ing strong, ____   play - ing my fa - v'rite
said, "Can I take you home ____   where we can be a -

song,   and I could tell it would - n't be long ____
lone?"   And next, we were mov - ing

99

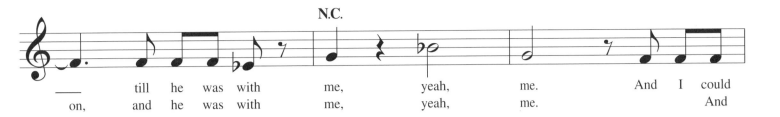

till he was with me, yeah, me. And I could
on, and he was with me, yeah, me. And

tell it would-n't be long ___ till he was with me, yeah,
next, we were mov-ing on, and he was with me, yeah,

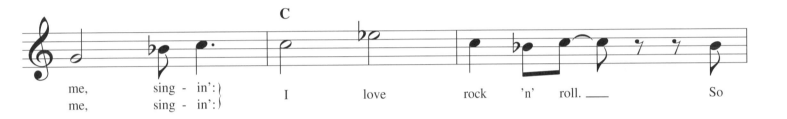

me, sing - in': ⎱ I love rock 'n' roll. ___ So
me, sing - in': ⎰

put an-oth-er dime in the juke-box, ba - by. I love

rock 'n' roll. ___ So come and take your time and dance with

me. He I said, "Can I take you home ___

100

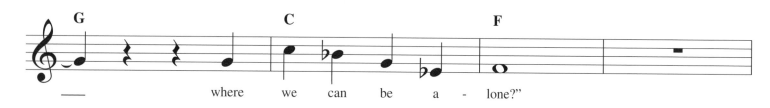

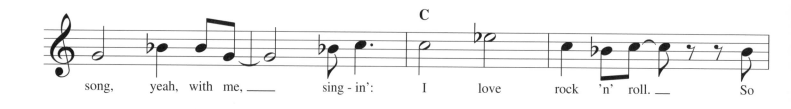

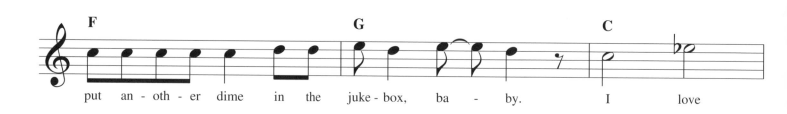

I'LL TAKE YOU THERE

Words and Music by
ALVERTIS ISBELL

Moderately

Female: I know a place, ya'll, _____ ain't no-bod - y ____

____ cry - in', no, _____ ain't no-bod-y _____ wor - ried.

Oh, ain't no smil - ing _____ fac - es _____ ly - ing to the

rac - es. Male: I said ain't ____ no smil - ing fac - es, no smil -

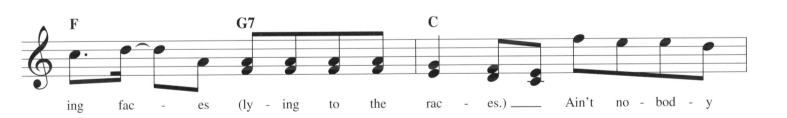

ing fac - es (ly - ing to the rac - es.) ____ Ain't no-bod - y

cry - ing, ___ no more cry - ing. ___ If you're read - y now, ___

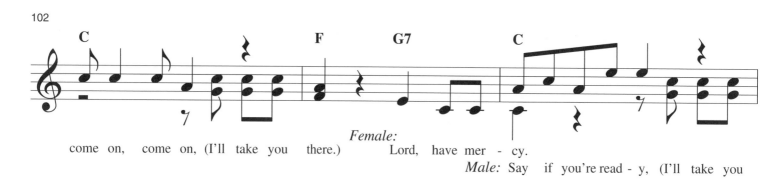

come on, come on, (I'll take you there.) *Female:* Lord, have mer - cy.
Male: Say if you're read - y, (I'll take you

there.) Oh, _____ yeah. Help me, help me. (I'll take you

there.) Come on, I said come on, _____ (I'll take you there.)
Help _____ me. __

(Instrumental)   *Female:* If you're read - y now.

Female: Oh, I, _____ oh, I, _____ I know __

____ a place, ____ ya'll, oh, there ain't no - bod - y cry-ing.

JOLENE

Words and Music by
DOLLY PARTON

Moderately slow

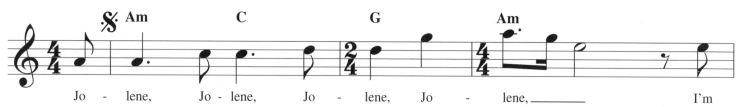

Jo - lene, Jo - lene, Jo - lene, Jo - lene, _____ I'm

beg - ging of you, please don't take my man. _____ Jo -

lene, Jo - lene, Jo - lene, Jo - lene, _____ please don't take him just be - cause you

can. _____ Your beau - ty is be - yond com - pare, with
You could have your choice of men, but

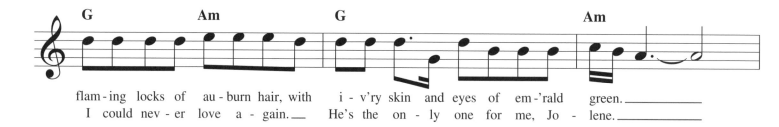

flam - ing locks of au - burn hair, with i - v'ry skin and eyes of em - 'rald green. _____
I could nev - er love a - gain. _ He's the on - ly one for me, Jo - lene. _____

Your smile is like a breath of spring, your voice is soft like sum - mer rain, and
I had to have this talk with you; my hap - pi - ness de - pends on you and

To Coda ⊕

I can - not com - pete with you, ___ Jo - lene. He
what - ev - er you de - cide to do, ___ Jo - lene. Jo -

talks a-bout you in his sleep and there's noth-ing I can do to keep from cry-in' when he calls your name, Jo-

lene._____ And I can eas-'ly un-der-stand how you could eas-'ly take my man, but you

don't know what he means to me, Jo - lene. Jo -

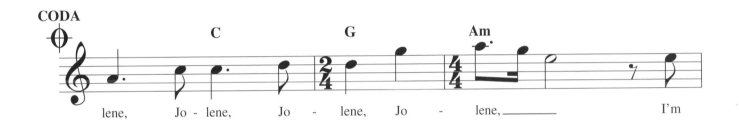

CODA

lene, Jo - lene, Jo - lene, Jo - lene,_____ I'm

beg-ging of you, please don't take my man.____ Jo - lene, Jo - lene, Jo-

lene, Jo - lene,____ please don't take him just be-cause you can._____

___ Jo - lene, Jo - lene, please don't take my man, Jo - lene, Jo-

lene, Jo - lene. My hap-pi-ness de-pends on you, Jo - lene.

KANSAS CITY

Words and Music by JERRY LEIBER
and MIKE STOLLER

Bright Shuffle

I'm go-in' to Kan-sas Cit-y, Kan-sas Cit-y here I come.

I'm go-in' to Kan-sas Cit-y, Kan-sas Cit-y here I come.

They got a cra-zy way of lov-in' there and I'm gon-na get me some.

I'm gon-na be stand-in' on the cor-ner Twelfth Street and Vine.
pack my clothes, leave at the crack of dawn.

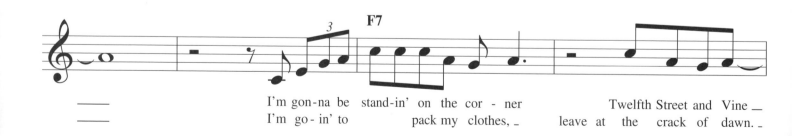

I'm gon-na be stand-in' on the cor-ner Twelfth Street and Vine.
I'm go-in' to pack my clothes, leave at the crack of dawn.

LA BAMBA

By RITCHIE VALENS

Moderate Latin Rock

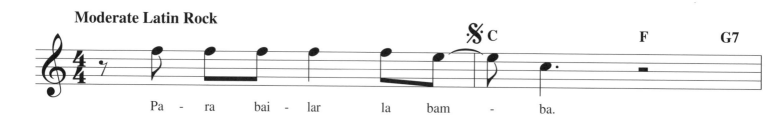

Pa - ra bai - lar la bam - ba.

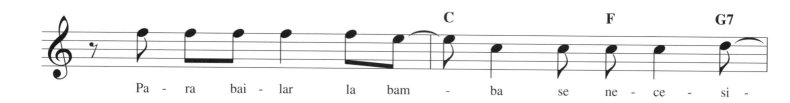

Pa - ra bai - lar la bam - ba se ne - ce - si -

- ta u - na po - ca de gra - cia.

U - na po - ca de gra - cia pa' mi pa' ti ____

____ y ar - ri - ba ar - ri - ba;

ar - ri - ba ar - ri - ba por ti se re ____

por ti se re se re. Yo no soy ma - ri -

ne - ro. Yo no soy ma - ri - ne - ro, soy ca - pi - tan;

To Coda

yo no soy ma - ri - ne - ro, soy ca - pi - tan.

Bam - ba bam - ba, bam - ba bam -

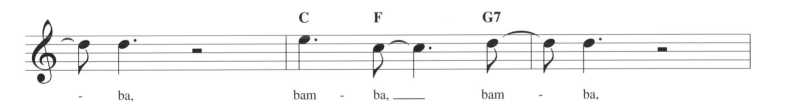

- ba, bam - ba, bam - ba,

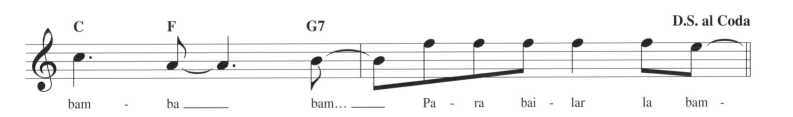

D.S. al Coda

bam - ba bam... Pa - ra bai - lar la bam -

CODA

Repeat and Fade

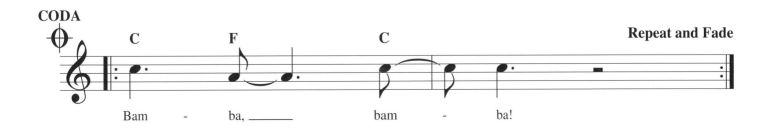

Bam - ba, bam - ba!

LAST TRAIN TO CLARKSVILLE

Words and Music by BOBBY HART
and TOMMY BOYCE

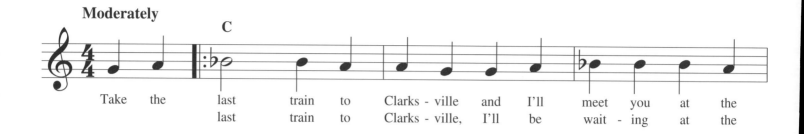

Take the last train to Clarks - ville and I'll meet you at the
last train to Clarks - ville, I'll be wait - ing at the

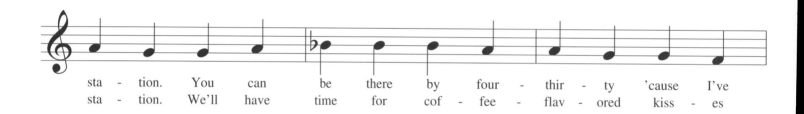

sta - tion. You can be there by four - thir - ty 'cause I've
sta - tion. We'll have time for cof - fee - flav - ored kiss - es

made your res - er - va - tion. Don't be slow, _____ oh, no, no, no. _____
and a bit of con - ver - sa - tion. Oh, _____ oh, no, no, no. _____

_____ Oh, no, no, no. _____ 'Cause I'm
_____ Oh, no, no, no. _____ Take the

leav - ing in the morn - ing and I must see you a -
last _____ train to Clarks - ville, now I must hang up the

111

gain;   we'll have   one more night to - geth - er 'til the
phone;   I can't   hear you in this nois - y rail - road

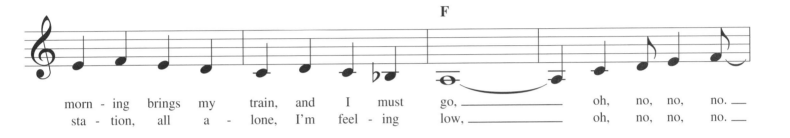

morn - ing brings my train, and I must go, _____ oh, no, no, no. ___
sta - tion, all a - lone, I'm feel - ing low, _____ oh, no, no, no. ___

_____ Oh, no, no, no. _____ And I
_____ Oh, no, no, no. _____ And I

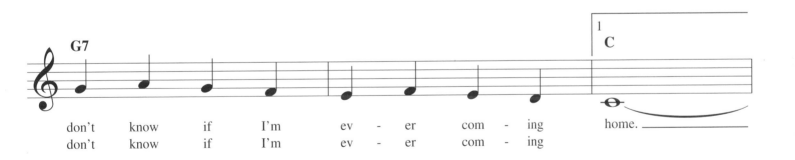

don't know if I'm ev - er com - ing home. _____
don't know if I'm ev - er com - ing

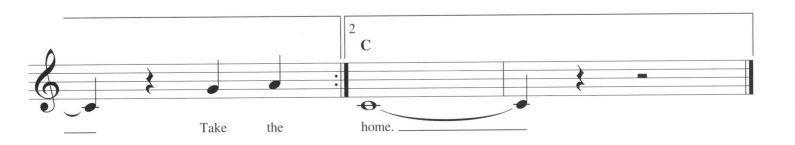

_____ Take the home. _____

LAY DOWN SALLY

Words and Music by ERIC CLAPTON,
MARCY LEVY and GEORGE TERRY

Brightly

There is noth - ing that _____ is wrong _____ in
sun ain't near - ly on _____ the rise, _____ and
long to see _____ the morn - ing light _____

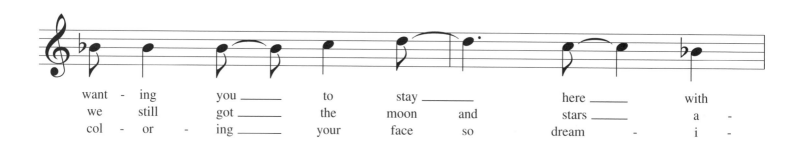

want - ing you _____ to stay _____ here _____ with
we still got _____ the moon and stars _____ a -
col - or - ing _____ your face so dream - i -

me. I know you've got _____ some - where _____
bove. Un - der - neath the vel -
ly. So don't you go _____ and say _____

_____ to go, _____ but won't you make _____ your - self
- vet skies, _____ love is all _____ that mat -
_____ good - bye; _____ you can lay _____ your wor -

_____ at home _____ and stay with me? _____ And don't you
- ters. Won't _____ you stay with me? _____ And don't you
- ries down _____ and stay with me. _____ And don't you

113

LEAVING ON A JET PLANE

Words and Music by
JOHN DENVER

115

LONELY STREET

Words and Music by CARL BELEW,
W.S. STEVENSON and KENNY SOWDER

I'm look - ing for that lone - ly street; I've got a sad, sad

tale to tell. I need a place to go and weep.

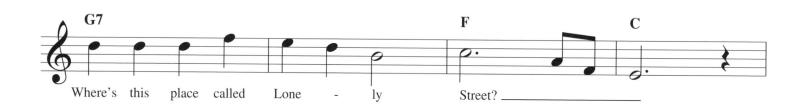

Where's this place called Lone - ly Street? ____

A place where there's just lone - li - ness, where dim lights bring for -

get - ful - ness, where bro - ken dreams and mem - 'ries meet.

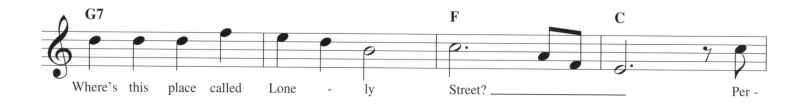

Where's this place called Lone - ly Street? ____ Per -

haps up - on that lone - ly street, there's some - one such as

I who came to bur - y bro - ken dreams and

watch an old ____ love ____ die. _____ If I could find that

lone - ly street, where dim lights bring for - get - ful - ness,

where bro - ken dreams and mem -'ries meet. Where's this place called

Lone - ly Street? _____

LONG TALL SALLY

Words and Music by ENOTRIS JOHNSON,
RICHARD PENNIMAN and ROBERT BLACKWELL

LOUIE, LOUIE

Words and Music by
RICHARD BERRY

LOVE ME DO

Words and Music by JOHN LENNON
and PAUL McCARTNEY

Love, love me do, _____ you know I love you. _____

_____ I'll al - ways be true. _____ So

please _____ love me do. _____

Whoa. _____ Love _____ me do. _____

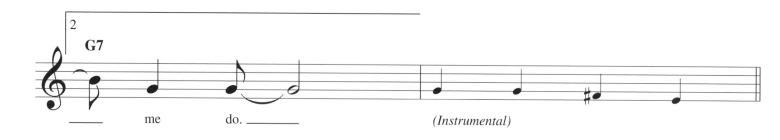

_____ me do. _____ (Instrumental)

Some - one to love, some - bod - y

Instrumental

MAKE THE WORLD GO AWAY

Words and Music by
HANK COCHRAN

NO PARTICULAR PLACE TO GO

Words and Music by
CHUCK BERRY

MAMA TRIED

Words and Music by
MERLE HAGGARD

The first thing I re - mem - ber know - in' was a lone - some whis - tle

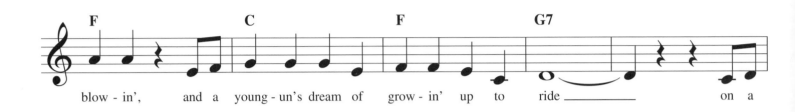

blow - in', and a young - un's dream of grow - in' up to ride _____ on a

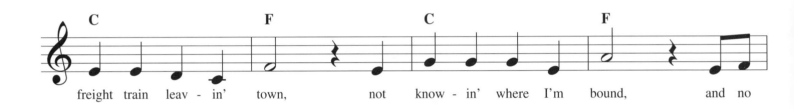

freight train leav - in' town, not know - in' where I'm bound, and no

one could change my mind, but Ma - ma tried. _____ One and

on - ly reb - el child, from a fam - 'ly meek and mild, my
Dad - dy, rest his soul, left my mom a heav - y load. She

ma - ma seemed to know what lay in store. _____ 'Spite of
tried so ver - y hard to fill his shoes. _____ Work - in'

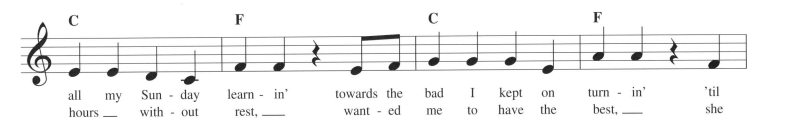

all my Sun - day learn - in' towards the bad I kept on turn - in' 'til
hours __ with - out rest, __ want - ed me to have the best, __ she

Ma - ma could - n't hold me an - y - more. _____ And I turned
tried to raise me right, but I re - fused. _____

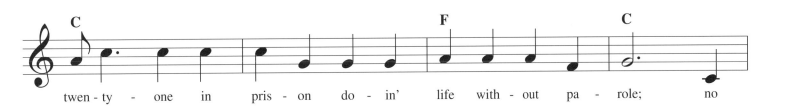

twen - ty - one in pris - on do - in' life with - out pa - role; no

one could steer me right, but Ma - ma tried, Ma - ma tried. Ma - ma

tried to raise me bet - ter, but her plead - ing I de - nied. That leaves on - ly me to

blame, 'cause Ma - ma tried. _____ Dear ol' tried. _____

ME AND BOBBY McGEE

Words and Music by KRIS KRISTOFFERSON
and FRED FOSTER

Moderately

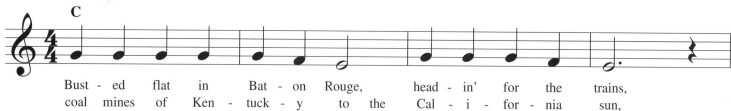

Bust - ed flat in Bat - on Rouge, head - in' for the trains,
coal mines of Ken - tuck - y to the Cal - i - for - nia sun,

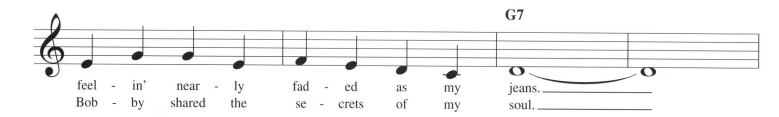

feel - in' near - ly fad - ed as my jeans.
Bob - by shared the se - crets of my soul.

Bob - by thumbed a die - sel down just be - fore it rained,
Stand - in' right be - side me, Lord, through ev - 'ry - thing I done,

took us all the way to New Or - leans.
and ev - 'ry night she kept me from the cold. Then

I took my har - poon out of my dirt - y red ban - dan - na and was
some - where near Sa - lin - as, Lord, I let her slip a - way,

blow - in' sad while Bob - by sang the blues. With them
look - in' for the home I hope she'll find. And I'd trade

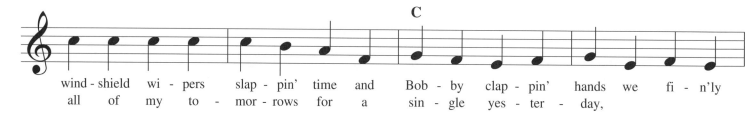

wind - shield wi - pers slap - pin' time and Bob - by clap - pin' hands we fi - n'ly
all of my to - mor - rows for a sin - gle yes - ter - day,

127

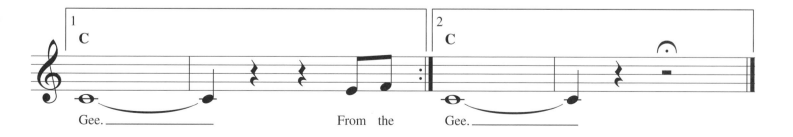

MELLOW YELLOW

Words and Music by
DONOVAN LEITCH

Moderately slow

I'm just mad a - bout Saf - fron, _____ Saf - fron's mad a - bout me. _
I'm just mad a - bout Four - teen, _____ Four - teen's mad a - bout me. _
Born high for - ev - er to _____ fly, _____ wind ve - loc - i - ty: nill. _
Instrumental

_____ _____ _____ I'm - a just mad a - bout Saf - fron, _____
I'm - a just mad a - bout Four - teen, _____
Born _ high for - ev - er to _____ fly, _____

she's just mad a - bout me. _____ }
she's just mad a - bout me. _____ }   They call me Mel - low Yel - low. _____ *(Spoken:)* *Quite rightly.*
if you want your cup I will fill. _____ }

(4.) *(Instrumental continues)*

They call me Mel - low Yel - low. _____ *Quite rightly.*   They call me Mel - low

1, 2, 4   **G**   **To Coda** ⊕
(last time)

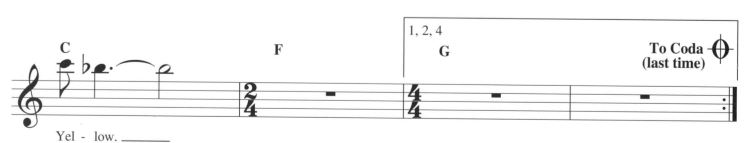

Yel - low. _____
(4.) *(End instrumental)*

MONEY
(That's What I Want)

Words and Music by BERRY GORDY
and JANIE BRADFORD

Heavy Rock

(Instrumental)

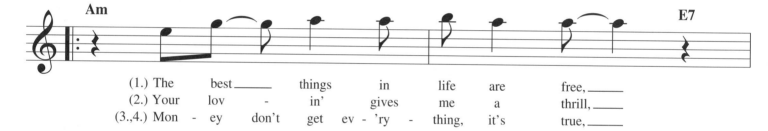

(1.) The best_____ things in life are free,_____
(2.) Your lov - in' gives me a thrill,_____
(3.,4.) Mon - ey don't get ev - 'ry - thing, it's true,_____

but you can keep 'em for the birds and bees._____ Now give me
but your lov - in' don't pay my bills._____ Now give me
what it don't get, I_____ can't use._____ Now give me

mon - ey, that's what I want,

that's what I want_____ yeah,_____

131

MONY, MONY

Words and Music by BOBBY BLOOM, TOMMY JAMES,
RITCHIE CORDELL and BO GENTRY

Moderately

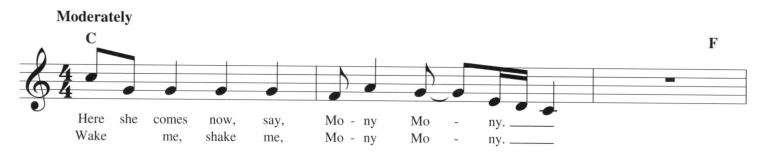

Here she comes now, say, Mo-ny Mo-ny. _____
Wake me, shake me, Mo-ny Mo-ny. _____

Shoot 'em down, turn a-round, come on, Mo-ny. _____
Shot-gun get it done, come on, Mo-ny. _____

Hey, she give me lov-in', I feel _____
Don't stop look-in', it feels _____

_____ all right _____ now. _____ You've got me
_____ so good, _____ yeah. _____

toss-in', turn-in' the mid-dle of the night, and I feel _____ all right. _____ I say Yeah! _____
Don't stop now. Come on, Mo-ny. _____ Come on, Mo-ny, Yeah! _____

_____ (Yeah!) _____ Yeah! _____ (Yeah!) _____ Yeah! _____ (Yeah!) Yeah! _____ (Yeah!) Yeah! _____

(Yeah!) Yeah! ___ You make me feel (Mo - ny Mo - ny)

so (Mo - ny Mo - ny) good. (Mo - ny Mo - ny) Yeah! (Mo - ny Mo - ny)

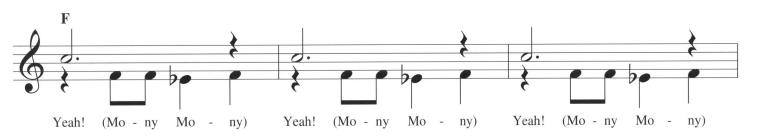

Yeah! (Mo - ny Mo - ny) Yeah! (Mo - ny Mo - ny) Yeah! (Mo - ny Mo - ny)

Yeah! (Mo - ny Mo - ny) Yeah! ___ (Yeah!) _ Yeah! ___ (Yeah!) _ Yeah! ___

___ (Yeah!) Yeah! _ (Yeah) Yeah! ___ (Yeah!) Yeah! _ (Yeah!)

OLD TIME ROCK & ROLL

Words and Music by GEORGE JACKSON
and THOMAS E. JONES III

Moderate Rock 'n' Roll beat

Just take those old rec-ords off the shelf. __ I'll sit and lis-ten to 'em
tan - go. _____ I'd rath - er hear some blues or

by my - self. __ To-day's mu - sic ain't got the same soul.
funk - y old soul. There's on - ly one sure way to get me to go;

I like that old - time __ rock 'n' roll. __ Don't try to take me to a
start play-ing old - time __ rock 'n' roll. __ Call me a re - lic. Call me

dis - co. You'll nev - er e - ven get me out on the floor. __
what you will. Say I'm old - fash-ioned. Say I'm o - ver the hill. __

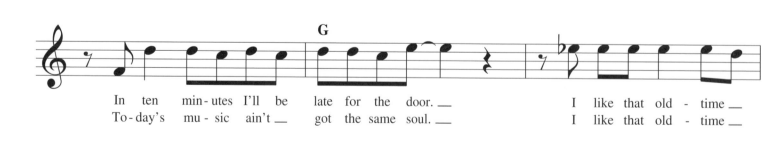

In ten min-utes I'll be late for the door. __ I like that old - time __
To-day's mu - sic ain't __ got the same soul. __ I like that old - time __

rock 'n' roll. __ }
rock 'n' roll. __ } Still like that old - time __ rock 'n' roll. __

That kind of mu - sic just soothes my soul. __ I rem - i - nisce a - bout the

days of old __ with that old - time rock 'n' roll. __

(Instrumental)

Won't go to hear 'em play a

Still like that old - time __ rock 'n' roll. __ That kind of mu - sic just

soothes my soul. __ I rem - i - nisce a - bout the days of old __

with that old - time rock 'n' roll. __

PEPPERMINT TWIST

Words and Music by JOSEPH DiNICOLA
and HENRY GLOVER

RING OF FIRE

Words and Music by MERLE KILGORE
and JUNE CARTER

RESPECT

Words and Music by
OTIS REDDING

Moderate Rock

What you want,   ba - by, I got.
I ain't gon - na do you wrong   while you gone.

What you need,   you know I got it.
I ain't gon - na do you wrong   'cause I don't wan - na.

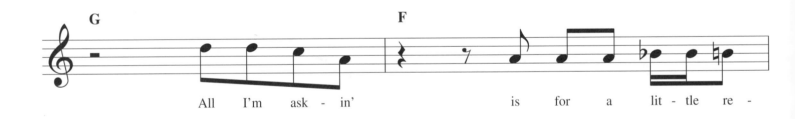

All I'm ask - in'   is for a lit - tle re -

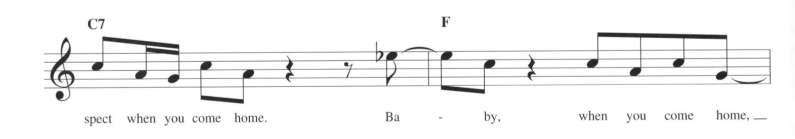

spect when you come home.   Ba - by, when you come home, ___

___   re - spect.

I'm out ___ to give you
Ooh, ___ your kiss - es,

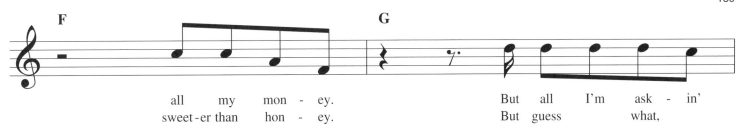

all my mon - ey.
sweet -er than hon - ey.
But all I'm ask - in'
But guess what,

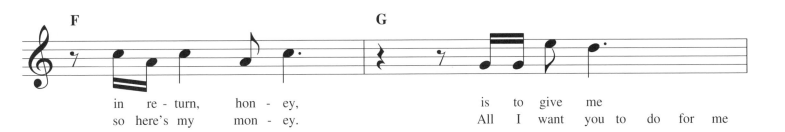

in re - turn, hon - ey,
so here's my mon - ey.
is to give me
All I want you to do for me

my pro - per re - spect }
is give me some here }
when you get home.
Yeah, ba - by, when you get

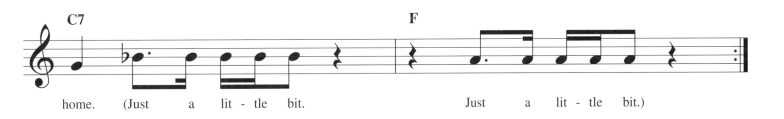

home. (Just a lit - tle bit.
Just a lit - tle bit.)

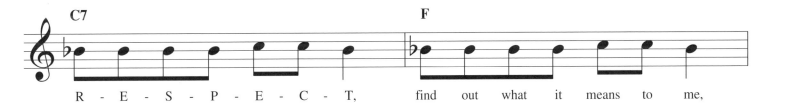

R - E - S - P - E - C - T,
find out what it means to me,

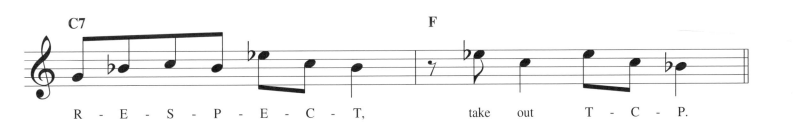

R - E - S - P - E - C - T,
take out T - C - P.

A lit - tle re - spect.

ROCK AROUND THE CLOCK

Words and Music by MAX C. FREEDMAN
and JIMMY DeKNIGHT

Moderately

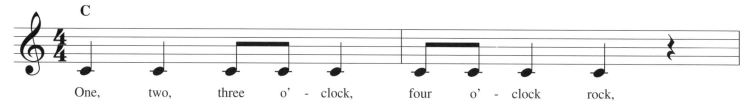

One, two, three o'-clock, four o'-clock rock,

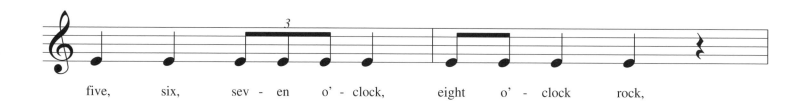

five, six, sev-en o'-clock, eight o'-clock rock,

nine, ten, e-lev-en o'-clock, twelve o'-clock rock, we're gon-na

rock a-round the clock to-night. _____ Put your

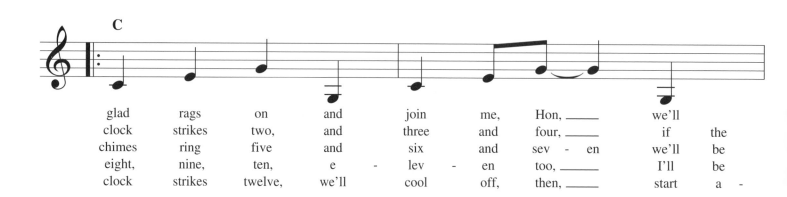

glad rags on and join me, Hon, _____ we'll
clock strikes two, and three and four, _____ if the
chimes ring five and six and sev-en we'll be
eight, nine, ten, e-lev-en too, _____ I'll be
clock strikes twelve, we'll cool off, then, _____ start a-

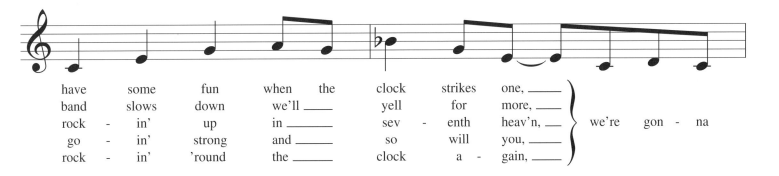

have some fun when the clock strikes one, ___
band slows down we'll ___ yell for more, ___
rock - in' up in ___ sev - enth heav'n, ___ } we're gon - na
go - in' strong and ___ so will you, ___
rock - in' 'round the ___ clock a - gain, ___

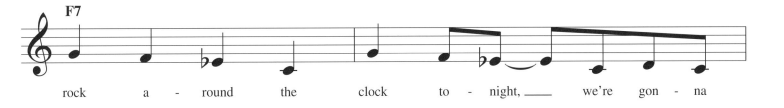

F7 rock a - round the clock to - night, ___ we're gon - na

C rock, rock, rock, 'til broad day - light, ___ we're gon - na

G7 rock, gon - na rock a - round ___ the clock ___ to - night. __

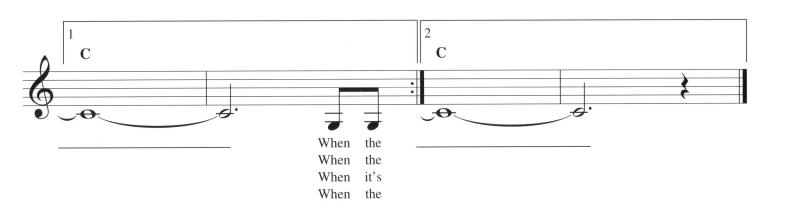

1 C ___

2 C

When the ___
When the
When it's
When the

ROUTE 66

By BOBBY TROUP

Moderately bright

If you ___ ev - er plan to mo - tor West ___ trav - el

my way, take the high - way that's the best. ___ Get your

kicks on Route ___ Six - ty - six! ___ It

winds ___ from Chi - ca - go to L. A. ___ More than

two ___ thou - sand miles all the way. ___ Get your

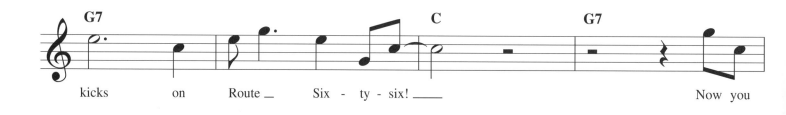

kicks on Route ___ Six - ty - six! ___ Now you

go thru Saint Loo-ey and Jop - lin, Mis-sou-ri and Ok-la-ho-ma Cit-y is might-

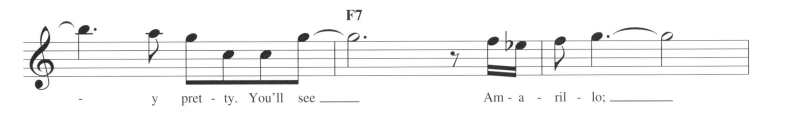

-y pret - ty. You'll see _____ Am - a - ril - lo; _____

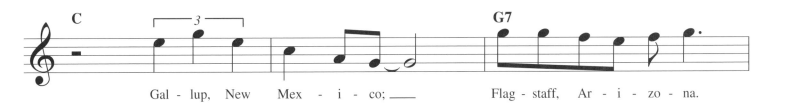

Gal - lup, New Mex - i - co; ___ Flag - staff, Ar - i - zo - na.

Don't for - get Wi - no - na, King - man, Bar - stow, San Ber - nar - di - no. Won't

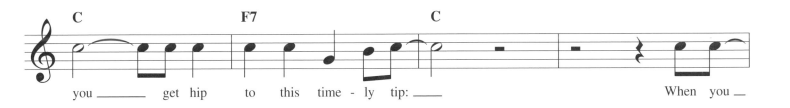

you _____ get hip to this time - ly tip: ___ When you _

_____ make that Cal - i - for - nia trip, ___ get your

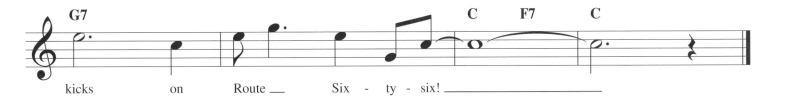

kicks on Route ___ Six - ty - six! _____

RUBY BABY

Words and Music by JERRY LEIBER
and MIKE STOLLER

Moderately

I love a girl and-a Ru-by is her name. ___
Each time I see you, ___ ba-by, my heart cries. ___

This girl don't ___ love me but I love her just the same. ___
Tell yuh, I'm gon-na steal ___ you a - way from all those guys. ___

Ru-by, Ru-by, how I want yuh, like a ghost I'm a
From the hap-py day I met yuh, I made a bet that I was

gon-na haunt yuh. Ru-by, Ru-by, Ru-by, will you be
gon-na get yuh. Ru-by, Ru-by, Ru-by, will you be

mine?
mine?   Ru-by, Ru-by, Ru-by, ba-by.

Ru-by, Ru-by, Ru-by, ba-by.   Ru-by, Ru-by,

C

Ru - by, ba - by.   Ru - by, Ru - by,   Ru - by, ba - by.

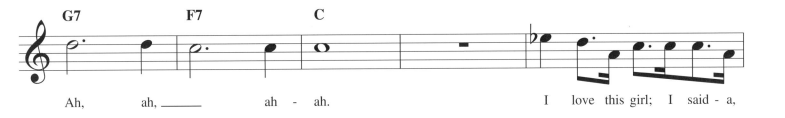

G7   **F7**   **C**

Ah,   ah, _____   ah - ah.   I love this girl; I said - a,

F7

Ru - by is her name. __   When this girl looks at me she just

C   **F7**

sets my heart a - flame. __   Got some hug - gin' and

C

kiss - es too, yeah, and I'm gon - na give them - a   all to you. Now lis - ten,

G7   **F**   **C**

Ru - by, Ru - by,   when will you be mine?

G7   **F7**   **C**

Ru - by, Ru - by,   when will you be mine? _____

SEARCHIN'

Words and Music by JERRY LEIBER
and MIKE STOLLER

Moderately

(Gon - na find her.)　　　　　(Gon - na find her.)

I been search - in',　　　　　uh huh

search - in',　　　oh yeah,　search - in' ev - 'ry

which _____ a - way. _____　Oh yeah, __ I been

search - in',　　　　search - in',

search - in' ev - 'ry which _____ a - way. _____

I'm like that North - west Mount - ie,

you know I'll bring her in _____ some day.

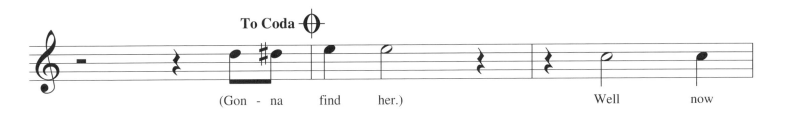

(Gon - na find her.) Well now

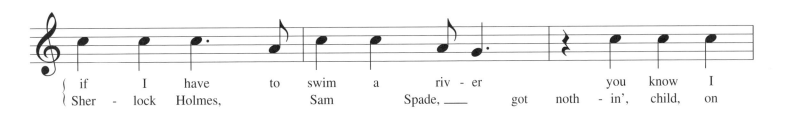

if I have to swim a riv - er you know I
Sher - lock Holmes, Sam Spade, _____ got noth - in', child, on

148

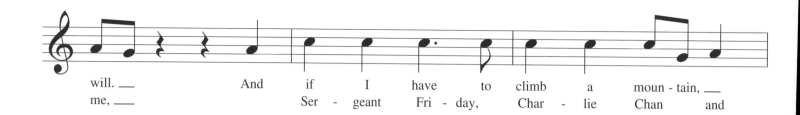

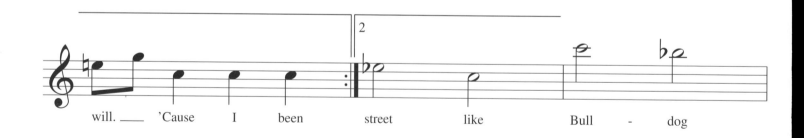

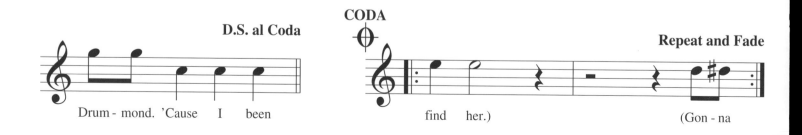

SAD SONGS

Words and Music by ELTON JOHN
and BERNIE TAUPIN

Moderately, with a Blues feel

Guess there are times _____ when we _____ all _____ need _____ to share _____ a lit -
suf - fer - in' _____ e - nough, _____ oh, _____ to write _

- tle pain _____ and iron - ing out the rough spots _____
_____ it down _____ when ev - 'ry sin - gle word makes sense, _____

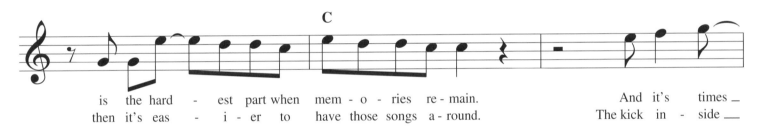

is the hard - est part when mem - o - ries re - main. And it's times _
then it's eas - i - er to have those songs a - round. The kick in - side _

_____ like these _ when we all _____ need _ to hear _ the ra - di - o, _____
_____ is in _____ the _____ line _____ that fi - nal - ly gets _____ to you. _

'cause from the lips _____ of _____ some _ old sing - er we can share the trou - bles
And it feels so good to hurt _ so bad _____ and suf - fer just e - nough to

we al - read - y know.
sing ___ the blues. ___
Turn 'em on, _____ turn 'em on,

___ turn on those sad songs. ___ When all hope is gone, ___

___ why don't you tune in and turn ___ them on? _____

They reach in - to your room, oh, _____ just feel ___ their ___ gen-

- tle touch. _ When all hope is gone, ___ a

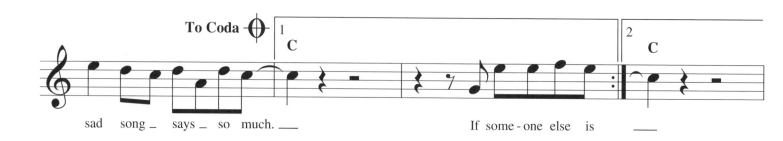

sad song _ says _ so much. ___ If some - one else is ___

151

Sad songs, ___ they ___ say, sad songs, ___ they ___

say. Sad songs, ___ they ___ say,

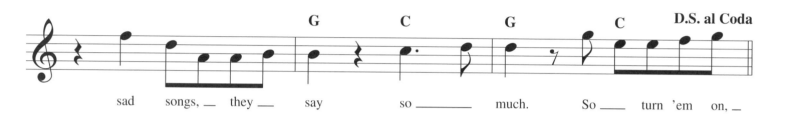

sad songs, ___ they ___ say so ___ much. So ___ turn 'em on, ___

___ When all hope is gone, ___ you know a

sad song ___ says ___ so much. ___ When ev-'ry lit-tle bit of

hope is gone, ___ you know a sad song ___ says ___ so much. ___

SEE YOU LATER, ALLIGATOR

Words and Music by
ROBERT GUIDRY

Medium Shuffle

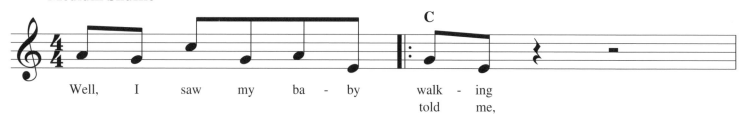

Well, I saw my ba - by walk - ing
told me,

with an - oth - er man to - day. _____
near - ly made me lose my head. _____

F7

Well, I saw my ba - by walk - ing
When I thought of what she told me,

C

with an - oth - er man to - day. _____
near - ly made me lose my head. _____

G7

When I asked her what's the mat - ter,
But the next time that I saw her,

C

this is what I heard her say.)
remind - ed her of what she said.)

See you lat - er, al - li - ga - tor,

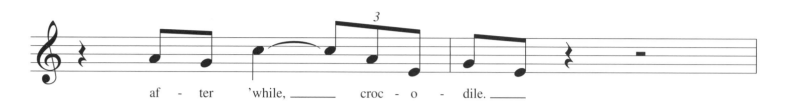

af - ter 'while, _____ croc - o - dile. _____

See you lat - er, al - li - ga - tor,

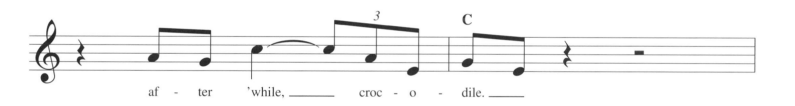

af - ter 'while, _____ croc - o - dile. _____

Can't you see you're in my way, now?

Don't you know you cramp my style?

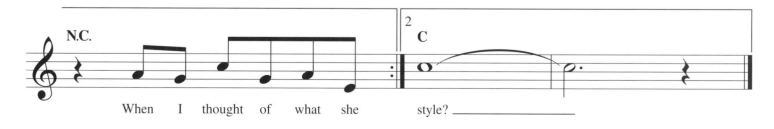

When I thought of what she style? _____

SEVEN BRIDGES ROAD

Words and Music by
STEPHEN T. YOUNG

Freely

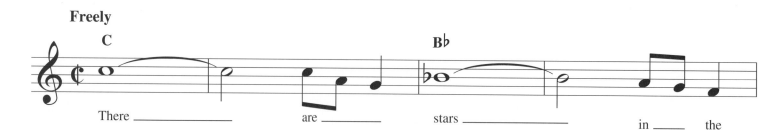

There _____ are _____ stars _____ in _____ the

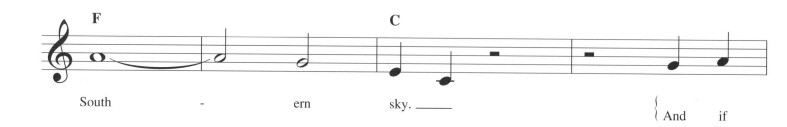

South - ern sky. _____ { And if

South - ward _____ as _____ you _____
ev - er _____ you de - cide _____ you should

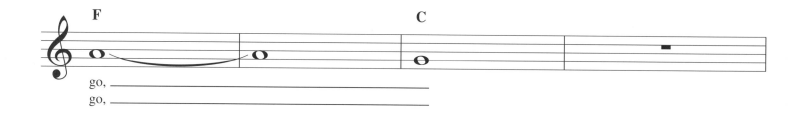

go, _____
go, _____

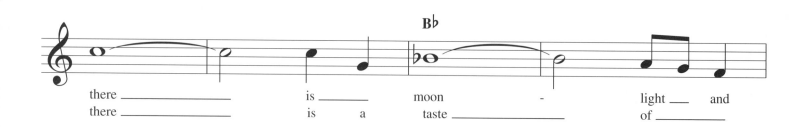

there _____ is _____ moon - light _____ and
there _____ is a taste _____ of

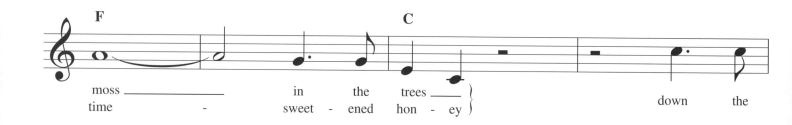

moss _____ in the trees _____ }
time - sweet - ened hon - ey } down the

TULSA TIME

Words and Music by
DANNY FLOWERS

SHE DON'T KNOW SHE'S BEAUTIFUL

Words and Music by BOB McDILL
and PAUL HARRISON

159

STIR IT UP

Words and Music by
BOB MARLEY

Moderate Reggae

Stir it up, ___
stir it up, ___   lit - tle dar - ling,   stir it up. ___

Come on and stir it up, ___   lit - tle dar - ling,

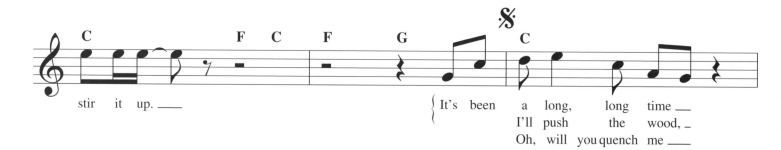

stir it up. ___
                    It's been a long, long time ___
                    I'll push the wood, _
                    Oh, will you quench me ___

since I've ___ got you on my mind.   And
I'll blaze ___ your fire,   then I'll sat - is - fy your,   your heart's de - sire.
while I'm ___ thirst - y?   Or would you cool me down   when I'm hot?

now you are ___ here,   I say it's so clear. ___   See what we can do, hon - ey,
Said I'll stir it, yeah,   ev - 'ry min - ute, yeah.   All you got to do, hon - ey,
Your rec - i - pe, dar - ling,   is so tast - y,   and you sure

just ___ me and ___ you. Come on and
                                            is ___ keep it in. And
                                            can ___ stir your pot. So   stir it up, ___

THE STROLL

Words and Music by CLYDE OTIS
and NANCY LEE

Moderate Rock beat

Come, let's stroll, _____ stroll a - cross the floor. ____
feel so good, _____ take me by the hand. ____

Come, let's stroll, _____ stroll a - cross the floor. ____
I feel so good, _____ take me by the hand. _

____ Now turn a - round, ba - by,
____ And let's ___ go stroll - ing

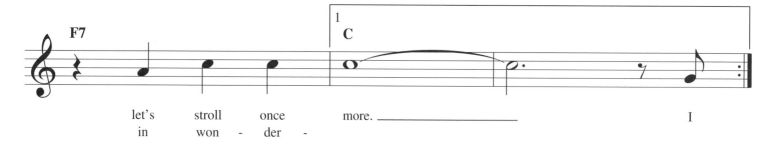

let's stroll once more. _____ I
in won - der -

land. _____ Stroll - ing, ____

____ stroll - ing, ____ rock and

roll - ing. Stroll - ing, ___

___ well - a rock - a my soul, how I love to

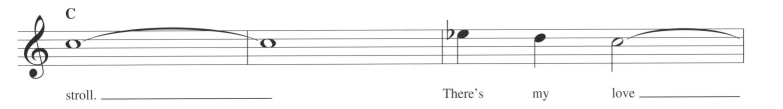

stroll. _____ There's my love _____

___ stroll - ing in the door. ___

There's my love _____ stroll - ing in the door. ___

___ Ba - by, let's go stroll - ing

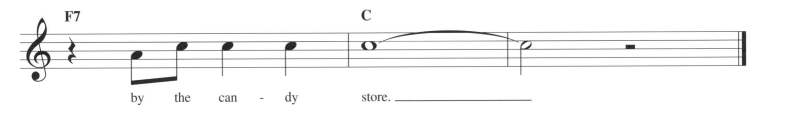

by the can - dy store. _____

STUCK ON YOU

Words and Music by AARON SCHROEDER
and J.L. McFARLAND

With a beat

You can shake an ap - ple off an ap - ple tree _____
Gon - na run my fin - gers thru your long black hair, _____

shake - a shake - a, sug - ar, but you'll nev - er shake me. _____ Uh - uh - uh. _____
squeeze _____ you _____ tight - er than a griz - zly bear. _____ Uh - huh - huh. _____

_____ No, sir - ee, _____ uh - uh. _____
_____ Yes, sir - ee, _____ uh - huh. _____

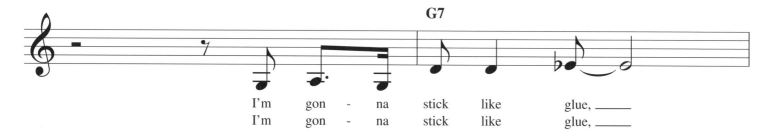

I'm gon - na stick like glue, _____
I'm gon - na stick like glue, _____

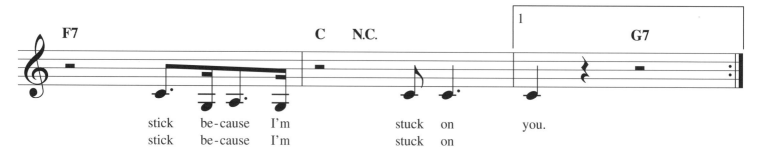

stick be - cause I'm stuck on you.
stick be - cause I'm stuck on

you.   Hide in the kitch - en, hide in the hall,

ain't gon - na do you no good at all. ___ 'Cause once I catch ya and the

kiss - in' starts, ___ a team o' wild hors - es could - n't tear us a - part.

Try to take a ti - ger from his dad - dy's side, ___

that's ___ how ___ love is gon - na keep us tied. ___ Uh - huh - huh. ___

___ Yes, sir - ee, ___ uh - huh. ___

___ I'm gon - na stick like glue, ___

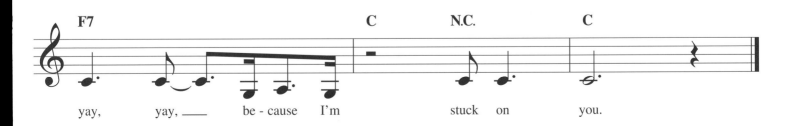

yay, yay, ___ be - cause I'm stuck on you.

SUNSHINE SUPERMAN

Words and Music by
DONOVAN LEITCH

Moderately, with a beat

Sun - shine ___ came soft - ly through my a - win-dow to - day. ___
Ev-ry' - bod - y's hus - tlin' just to have a lit - tle ___ scene. ___
Su - per-man or Green Lan - tern ain't got a - noth - in' on me. ___

___ Could -'ve tripped out eas - y a - but I've
___ When I say we'll be cool ___ I think that
___ I can make like a tur - tle and dive for

a - changed my ways. ___ It -'ll take time, __
you know what I mean. ___ We stood on a beach __
pearls in the sea. ___ A you- you-you can just sit ___

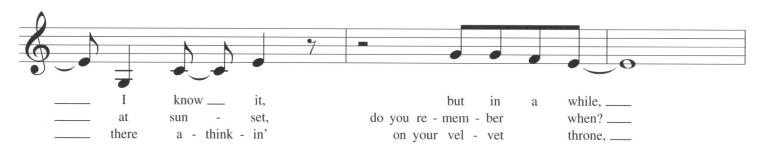

___ I know __ it, but in a while, ___
___ at sun - set, do you re - mem - ber when? ___
___ there a - think - in' on your vel - vet throne, ___

you're gon - na be mine, ___ I know it, we'll do it in style. _
I know a beach ___ where, ba - by, a - it nev - er ends. _
'bout all the rain - bows a - you can a - have for your own. _

___ 'Cause I made my mind up, you're
___ When you've made your mind up for -
___ When you've made your mind up for -

SURFIN' U.S.A.

Words and Music by
CHUCK BERRY

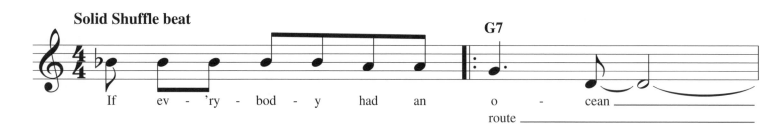

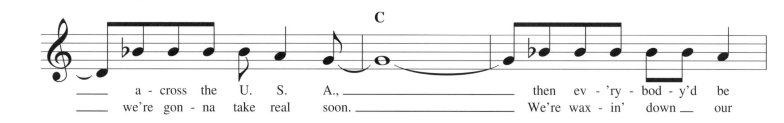

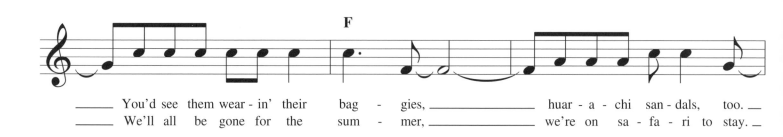

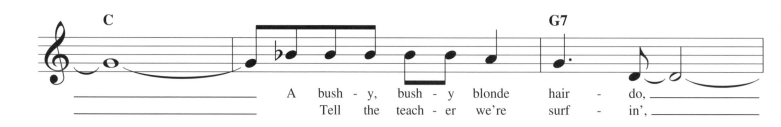

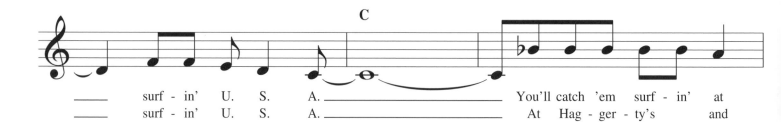

169

Del Mar, _____ Ven - tu - ra Coun - ty Line, _____
Swa - mi's, _____ Pa - cif - ic Pal - i - sades, _____

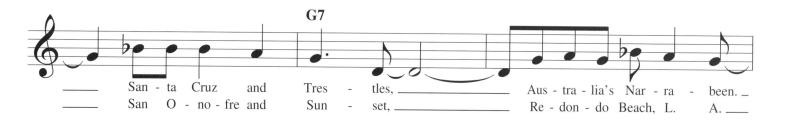

_____ San - ta Cruz and Tres - tles, _____ Aus - tra - lia's Nar - ra - been. _
_____ San O - no - fre and Sun - set, _____ Re - don - do Beach, L. A. ___

_____ All o - ver Man - hat - tan _____
_____ All o - ver La Jol - la, _____

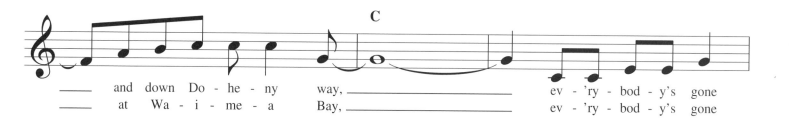

_____ and down Do - he - ny way, _____ ev - 'ry - bod - y's gone
_____ at Wa - i - me - a Bay, _____ ev - 'ry - bod - y's gone

surf - in', _____ surf - in' U. S. A. _____
surf - in', _____ surf - in' U. S. A. _____

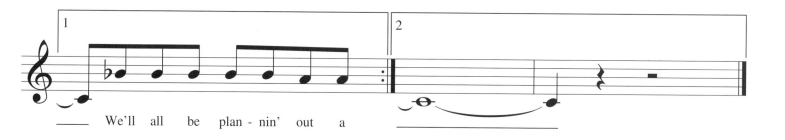

_____ We'll all be plan - nin' out a _____

(Let Me Be Your)
TEDDY BEAR

Words and Music by KAL MANN
and BERNIE LOWE

Medium bright Rock

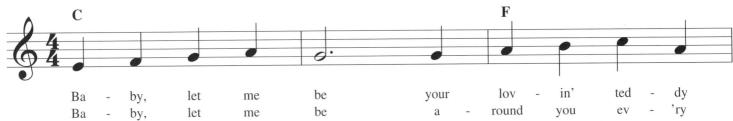

Ba - by, let me be your lov - in' ted - dy
Ba - by, let me be a - round you ev - 'ry

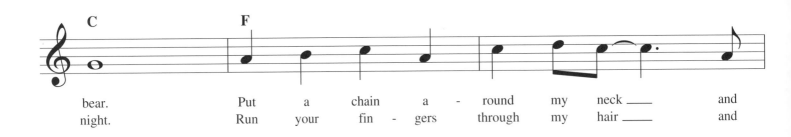

bear. Put a chain a - round my neck ____ and
night. Run your fin - gers through my hair ____ and

lead me an - y - where. } Oh, let me be ____
cud - dle me real tight. }

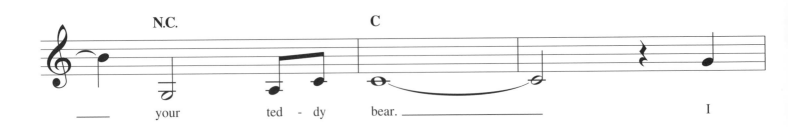

____ your ted - dy bear. ____ I

don't want to be your ti - ger 'cause ti - gers play too

rough. I don't want to be your li - on 'cause

li - ons ain't the kind you love e - nough.

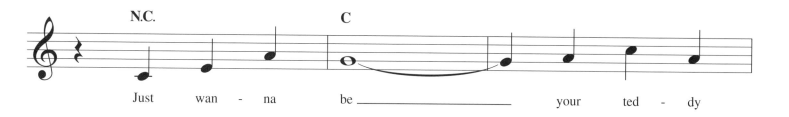

Just wan - na be _____ your ted - dy

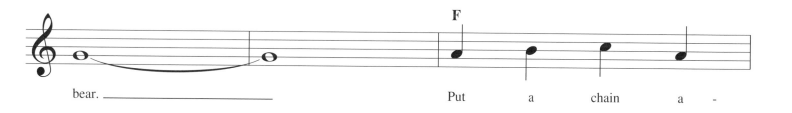

bear. _____ Put a chain a -

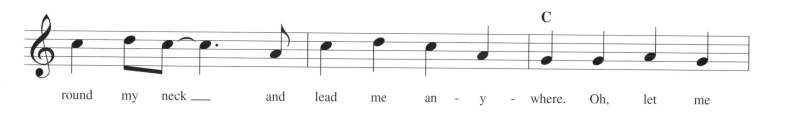

round my neck ___ and lead me an - y - where. Oh, let me

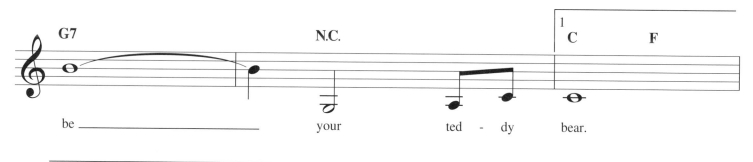

be _____ your ted - dy bear.

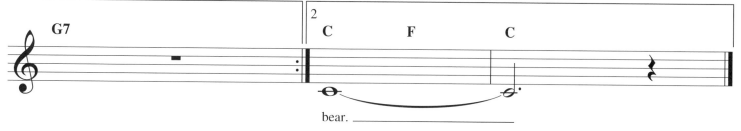

bear. _____

THESE BOOTS ARE MADE FOR WALKIN'

Words and Music by
LEE HAZLEWOOD

Brightly, with a beat

You keep say - in' you got some - thin' for me,
You keep ly - in' when you ought - a be truth - in',

some - thin' you call love, but con -
you keep los - in' when you ought - a not

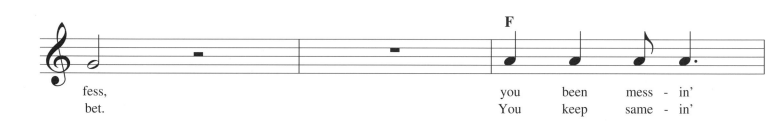

fess,   you been mess - in'
bet.   You keep same - in'

where you should - n't been mess - in'.   And now
when you ought - a be chang - in'.   Now what's

some - one else ____ is get - tin' all ____ your best.
right is right, ____ but you ain't been ____ right yet.

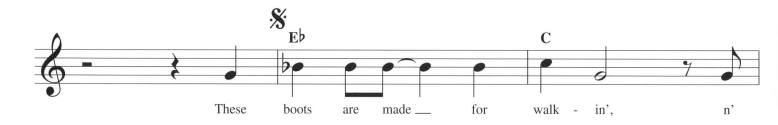

These boots are made ____ for walk - in', n'

THIS LAND IS YOUR LAND

Words and Music by
WOODY GUTHRIE

This land is your land _____ this land is my land _____

_____ from Cal - i - for - nia _____ to the New York is - land. _____

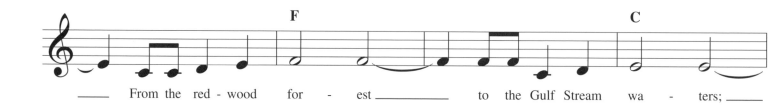

_____ From the red - wood for - est _____ to the Gulf Stream wa - ters;

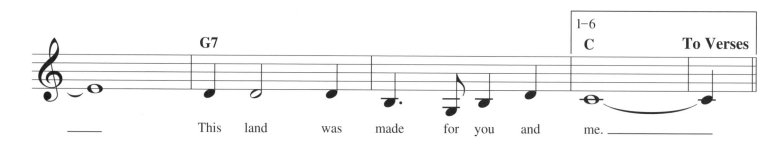

_____ This land was made for you and me. _____

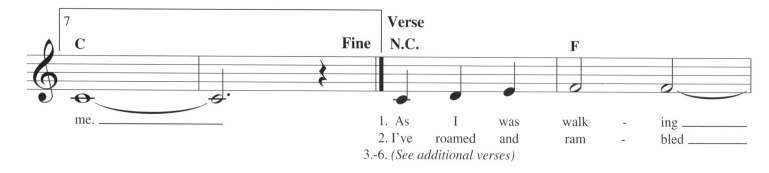

me. _____

1. As I was walk - ing _____
2. I've roamed and ram - bled _____
3.-6. *(See additional verses)*

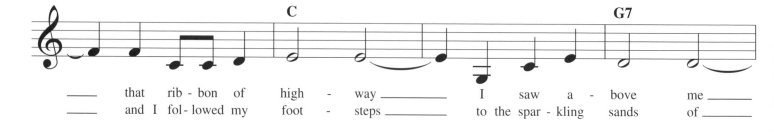

_____ that rib - bon of high - way _____ I saw a - bove me _____
_____ and I fol - lowed my foot - steps _____ to the spar - kling sands of _____

175

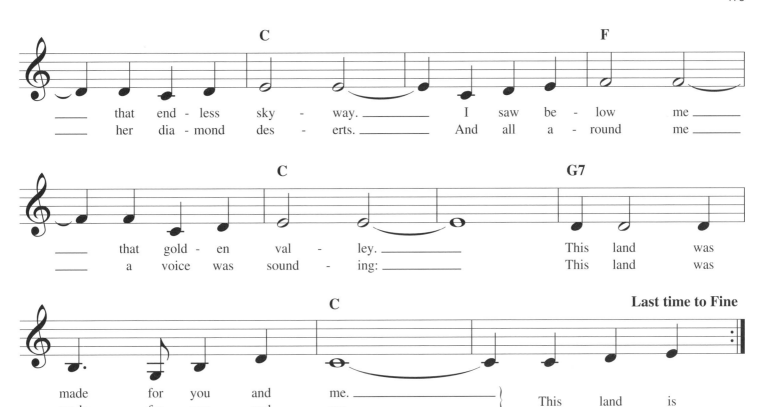

that end - less sky - way. _____ I saw be - low me _____
her dia - mond des - erts. _____ And all a - round me _____

that gold - en val - ley. _____ This land was
a voice was sound - ing: _____ This land was

made for you and me. _____
made for you and me. _____ } This land is

Last time to Fine

Additional Verses

3. When the sun came shining, and I was strolling,
   And the wheat fields waving, and the dust clouds rolling,
   As the fog was lifting, a voice was chanting:
   This land was made for you and me.
   Refrain

4. As I went walking, I saw a sign there,
   And on the sign it said, "No Trespassing,"
   But on the other side it didn't say nothing;
   That side was made for you and me.
   Refrain

5. In the shadow of the steeple, I saw my people.
   By the relief office, I saw my people.
   As they stood there hungry, I stood there asking:
   Is this land made for you and me?
   Refrain

6. Nobody living can ever stop me
   As I go walking that freedom highway.
   Nobody living can ever make me turn back;
   This land was made for you and me.
   Refrain

TOO MUCH

Words and Music by LEE ROSENBERG
and BERNARD WEINMAN

Medium Rock

Hon - ey, I _____ love you   too   much.
You spend all my mon - ey   too   much.
Ev - 'ry time I kiss your   sweet lips,

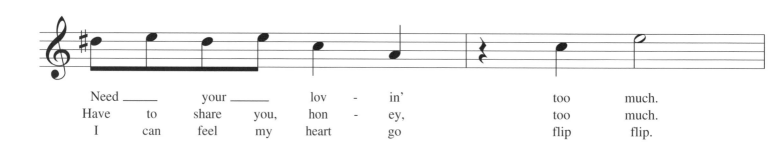

Need _____ your _____ lov - in'   too   much.
Have to share you, hon - ey,   too   much.
I can feel my heart go   flip   flip.

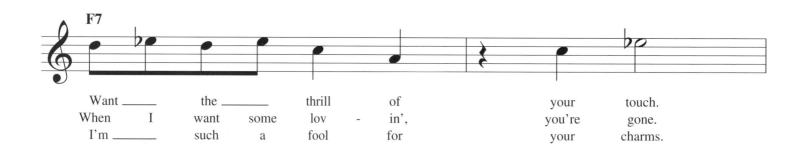

Want _____ the _____ thrill of   your   touch.
When I want some lov - in',   you're gone.
I'm _____ such a fool for   your   charms.

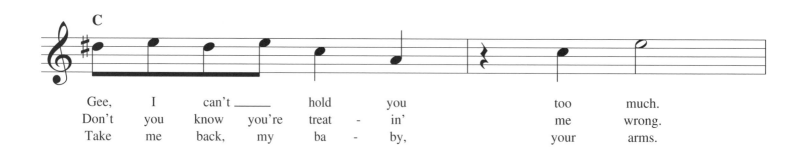

Gee, I can't _____ hold you   too   much.
Don't you know you're treat - in'   me   wrong.
Take me back, my ba - by,   your   arms.

You do all the liv - in' while I do all the giv - in' 'cause I
Now you got me start - ed, don't you leave me bro - ken - heart - ed 'cause I
Like to hear you sigh - in' e - ven though I know you're ly - in' 'cause I

TUTTI FRUTTI

Words and Music by LITTLE RICHARD PENNIMAN
and DOROTHY LA BOSTRIE

Bright Rock tempo

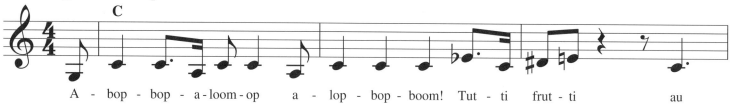

A - bop - bop - a - loom - op a - lop - bop - boom! Tut - ti frut - ti au

rut - ti, tut - ti frut - ti au rut - ti, tut - ti

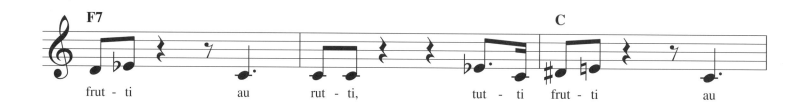

frut - ti au rut - ti, tut - ti frut - ti au

rut - ti, tut - ti frut - ti au rut - ti, a -

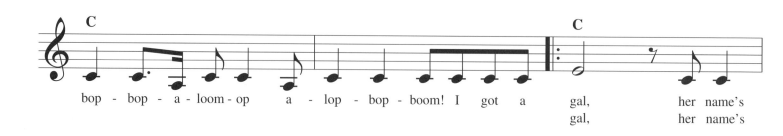

bop - bop - a - loom - op a - lop - bop - boom! I got a gal, her name's
gal, her name's

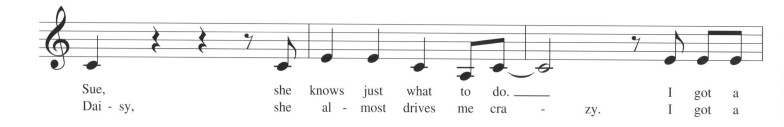

Sue, she knows just what to do. _____ I got a
Dai - sy, she al - most drives me cra - zy. I got a

THE TWIST

Words and Music by
HANK BALLARD

Rock 'n' Roll Shuffle

1. Come on, ba - by, _____ let's do _____ the
2.,3. *(See additional lyrics)*

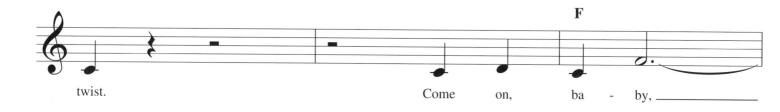

twist. Come on, ba - by, _____

_____ let's do the twist. Take me by my lit - tle

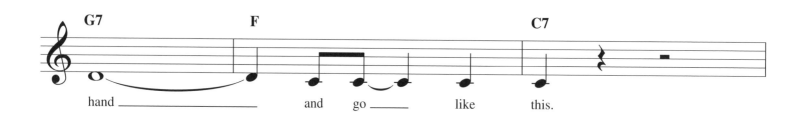

hand _____ and go _____ like this.

Chorus

Ee oh, twist, ba - by, ba - by,

twist. ('Round and a - round and a - round and a -) Just, _____

_____ just like this. ('Round and a - round) Come on, _____ lit - tle

miss, and do _____ the twist. ('Round and a -

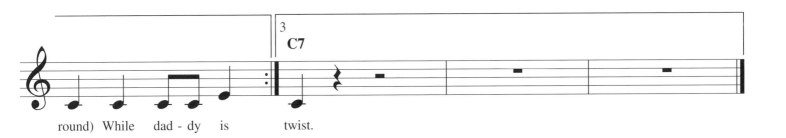

round) While dad - dy is twist.

Additional Lyrics

2. While daddy is sleeping and mama ain't around.
   While daddy is sleeping and mama ain't around.
   We're gonna twisty, twisty, twisty until we tear the house down.
   Chorus

3. You should see my little sis.
   You should see my little sis.
   She knows how to rock and she knows how to twist.
   Chorus

TWIST AND SHOUT

Words and Music by BERT RUSSELL
and PHIL MEDLEY

Moderately, with a beat

Well, shake it up, ba - by __ now, twist and shout!

Come on, come on, come on, ba - by __ now, come on and work it on out. __

Well, __ work it on out, __ you know you look so good. __
You know you twist, lit - tle girl, __ you know you twist so fine. __

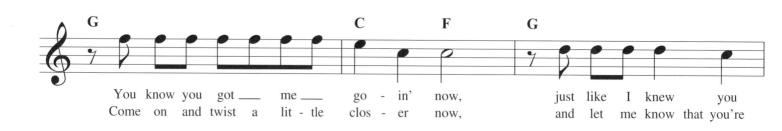

You know you got __ me __ go - in' now, just like I knew you
Come on and twist a lit - tle clos - er now, and let me know that you're

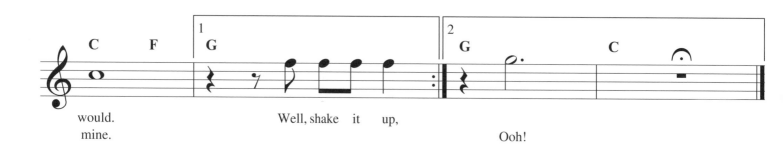

would. Well, shake it up,
mine. Ooh!

WHAT I GOT

Words and Music by BRAD NOWELL,
ERIC WILSON, FLOYD GAUGH
and LINDON ROBERTS

Moderate Rock

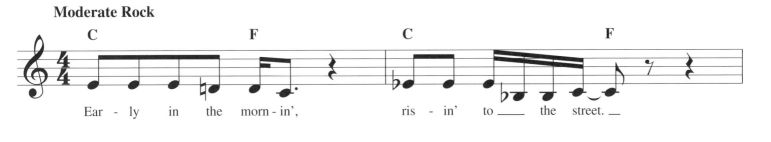

Ear - ly in the morn - in', ris - in' to ___ the street. ___

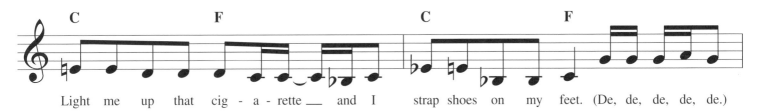

Light me up that cig - a - rette ___ and I strap shoes on my feet. (De, de, de, de, de.)

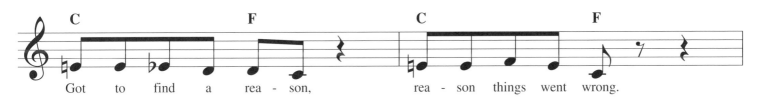

Got to find a rea - son, rea - son things went wrong.

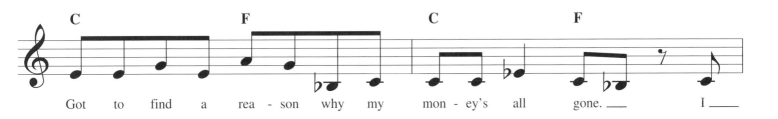

Got to find a rea - son why my mon - ey's all gone. ___ I ___

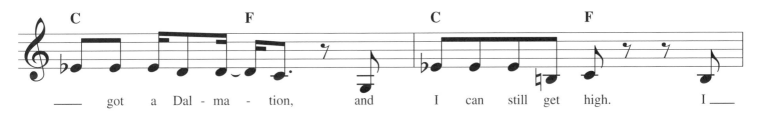

___ got a Dal - ma - tion, and I can still get high. I ___

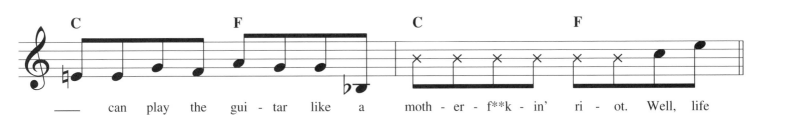

___ can play the gui - tar like a moth - er - f**k - in' ri - ot. Well, life

is (too short) so love the one you got 'cause you might get run o - ver or you might get shot.
Why, I don't cry when my dog runs _ a - way. I don't get an - gry at the bills I have to pay.

Nev - er start no stat - ic, I just get it off my (chest.) Nev - er had to bat - tle with no bul - let-proof _ (vest.)
I don't get an - gry when my mom smokes pot, hits the bot-tle and moves right to the rock.

Take a small ex-am-ple, take a ti - ti - ti-tip from me, _ Take all of your mon - ey, give it all... (to char - i - ty-ty.) Love
F**k-in' and fight-in', it's all the same. Liv-in' with Lou - ie Dog's the on-ly way to stay sane.

To Coda

is what I got, it's with-in my reach and the Sub-lime style's still straight _ from Long Beach. It all comes _
Let the lov-in', let the lov-in' come back __

__ back to you, you fi - n'ly get what you de - serve. Try and test that, you're bound to get served.

Love's what I got, don't start a ri - ot. You feel it when the dance gets hot.

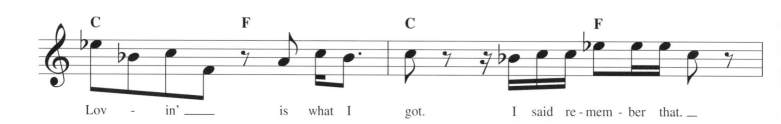

Lov - in' _____ is what I got. I said re-mem - ber that. _

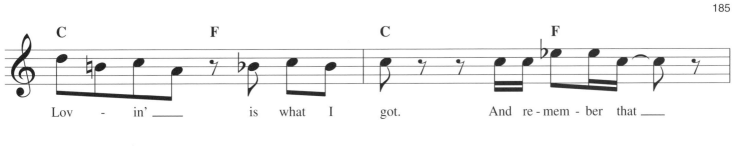

Lov - in' ____ is what I got. And re - mem - ber that ____

lov - in' ____ is what I got. I said re - mem - ber that ____

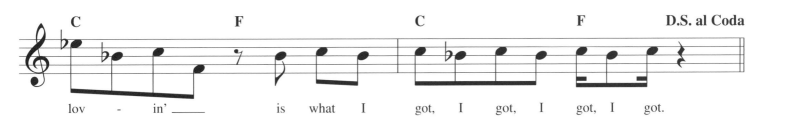

D.S. al Coda

lov - in' ____ is what I got, I got, I got, I got.

CODA

____ to me _____ 'Cause lov - in' ____ is what I

got. I said re - mem - ber that lov - in' ____ is what I

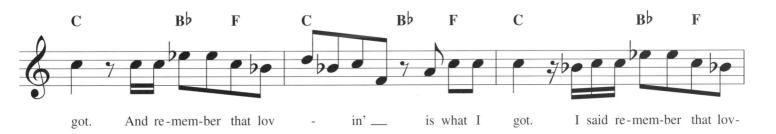

got. And re - mem - ber that lov - in' __ is what I got. I said re - mem - ber that lov-

- in' ____ is what I got, I got, I got, I got.

WHEN WILL I BE LOVED

Words and Music by
PHIL EVERLY

I've   been   cheat - ed, ____   been   mis -

treat - ed. _____   When   will   I _____   be ____

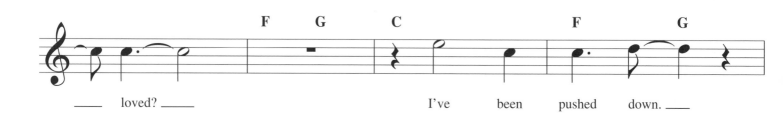

____ loved? ____   I've   been   pushed   down. ____

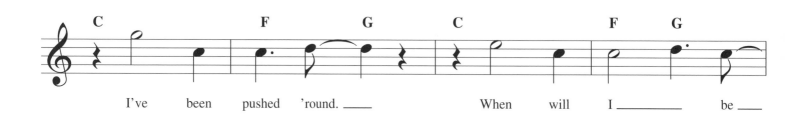

I've   been   pushed   'round. ____   When   will   I _____   be ____

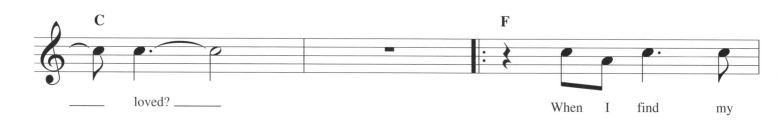

____ loved? ____   When   I   find   my

new   man ____   that   I   want   for   mine,   he

WHEN YOU SAY NOTHING AT ALL

Words and Music by DON SCHLITZ
and PAUL OVERSTREET

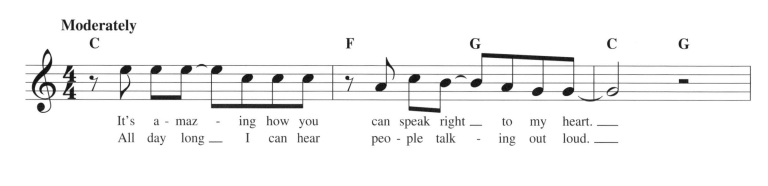

It's a - maz - ing how you can speak right __ to my heart. __
All day long __ I can hear peo - ple talk - ing out loud. __

With - out say - ing a word __ you can light up the dark. __
But when you __ hold me near __ you __ drown out the crowd. __

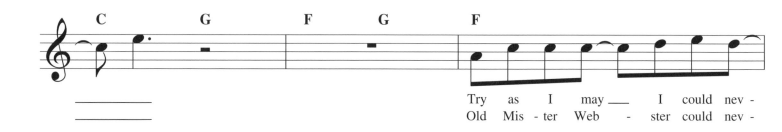

_____
_____
Try as I may __ I could nev -
Old Mis - ter Web - ster could nev -

- er ex - plain __ what I hear __ when you don't _____ say a thing. __
- er de - fine __ what's be - ing said __ be - tween your _____ heart and mine. __

__ } The smile on your face lets me know __ that you need __ me. There's a

truth in your eyes say - ing you'll __ nev - er leave __ me. A touch of your hand __ says you'll catch __

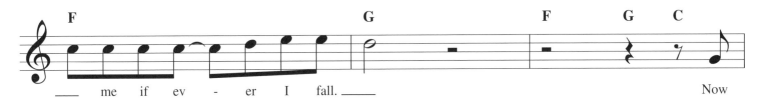

__ me if ev - er I fall. ___ Now

you say it best __ when you say noth - ing at all. ___ *(Instrumental)*

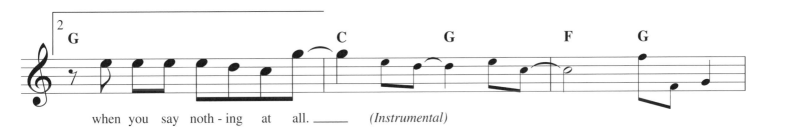

when you say noth - ing at all. ___ *(Instrumental)*

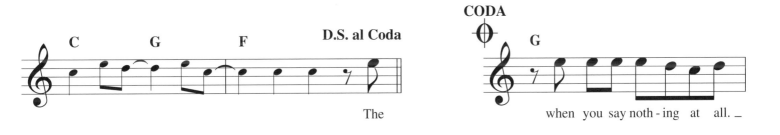

The   when you say noth - ing at all. _

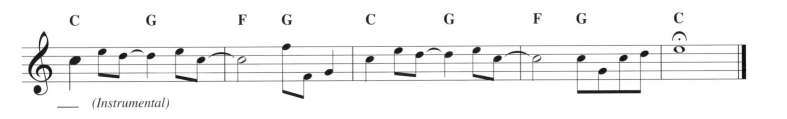

__ *(Instrumental)*

WHY DON'T WE DO IT IN THE ROAD

Words and Music by JOHN LENNON
and PAUL McCARTNEY

Moderately

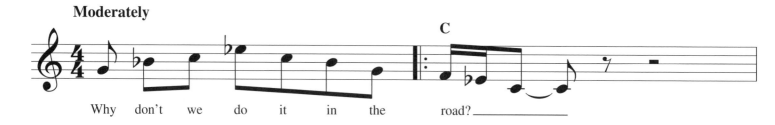

Why don't we do it in the road?

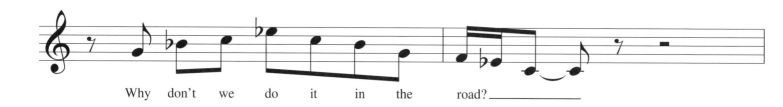

Why don't we do it in the road?

Why don't we do it in the road?

Why don't we do it in the road?

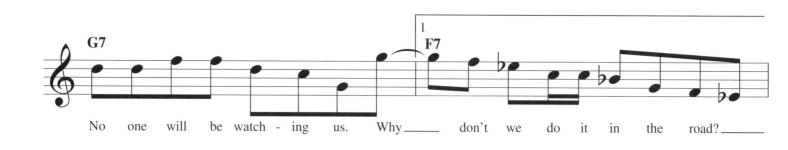

No one will be watch-ing us. Why don't we do it in the road?

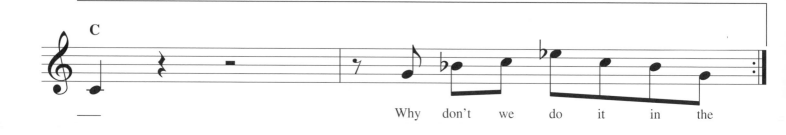

Why don't we do it in the

don't we do it in the road?_____ Oh._____

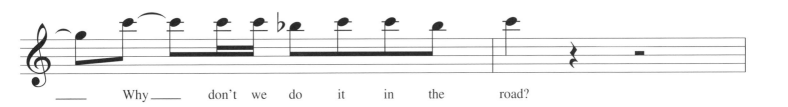

____ Why____ don't we do it in the road?

Why don't we do it in the road?_____

Why don't we do it, do it in the road?_____

Why don't we do it in the road?_____

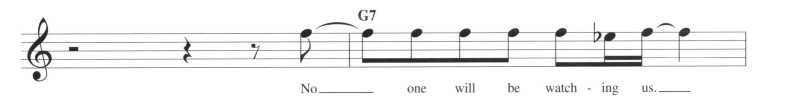

No_____ one will be watch - ing us.____

Why don't we do it in the road?

WILLIE AND THE HAND JIVE

Words and Music by
JOHNNY OTIS

Bright Rock

I know a cat named Way-Out Wil-lie. He got a
Pa - pa told Wil-lie, "You'll ru-in my home. He's
Ma - ma, ma-ma, look at Un-cle Joe. now
Doc-tor and a law-yer and an In-dian chief, They had a
Wil - lie and Mil-lie got mar-ried last fall.

cool lit-tle chick called Rock-in' Mil-lie. He can
You and that Hand-Jive has got to go." And
do - in' the Hand-Jive with sis-ter Flo.
they all dig that cra-zy beat. Well, the
lit-tle Wil-lie Jun-ior, and that ain't all.

walk and stroll and Su-sie Q. And
Wil - lie said, "Pa-pa, don't put me down. They're
Grand-ma gave ba - by sis-ter a dime. Said,
Way - Out Wil-lie gave 'em all a treat when he
ba - by got fa-mous in his crib, you see,

do that cra-zy Hand-Jive, too.
do - in' the Hand-Jive all o-ver town."
"Do that Hand-Jive one more time."
did that Hand-Jive with his feet.
do - in' the Hand-Jive on T - V.

Hand -

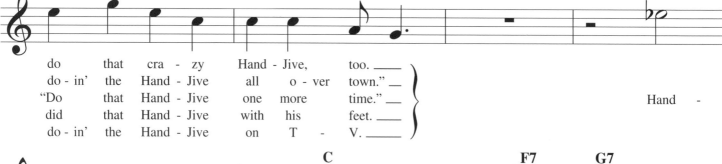

Jive.   Hand - Jive.   Hand - Jive.

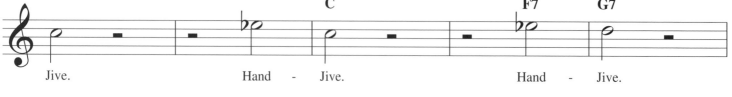

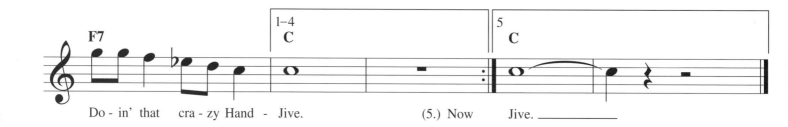

Do - in' that cra-zy Hand - Jive.   (5.) Now   Jive.

WOOLY BULLY

Words and Music by
DOMINGO SAMUDIO

Moderately

1. Mat - ty told Hat - ty _____ a - bout a thing she saw. _____
2., 3. (See additional lyrics)

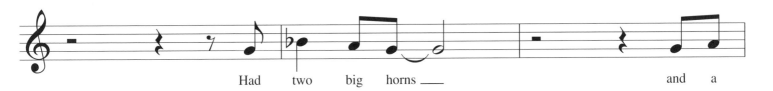

Had two big horns _____ and a

wool - ly jaw _____ Wool - y Bul - ly _____ Wool - y

Bul - ly _____ Wool - y Bul - ly _____ Wool - y

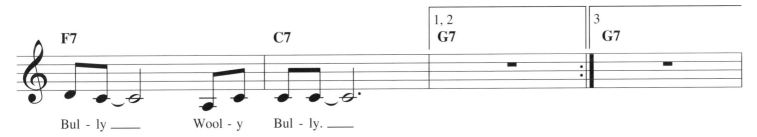

Bul - ly _____ Wool - y Bul - ly. _____

(Instrumental)

Additional Lyrics

2. Hatty told Matty
   Let's don't take no chance
   Let's not be L 7
   Come and learn to dance
   Wooly Bully - Wooly Bully -
   Wooly Bully - Wooly Bully - Wooly Bully.

3. Matty told Hatty
   That's the thing to do,
   Get yo' someone really
   To pull the wool with you -
   Wooly Bully - Wooly Bully
   Wooly Bully - Wooly Bully - Wooly Bully.

YOUR MAMA DON'T DANCE

Words and Music by JIM MESSINA
and KENNY LOGGINS

Moderate Rock Shuffle

Your ma - ma don't dance and your dad - dy don't rock and roll. ____

____ Your ma - ma don't dance and your

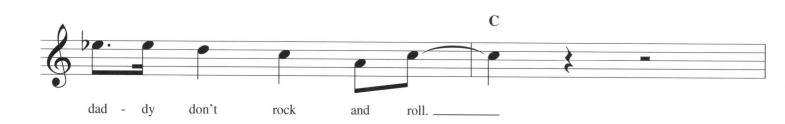

dad - dy don't rock and roll. _____

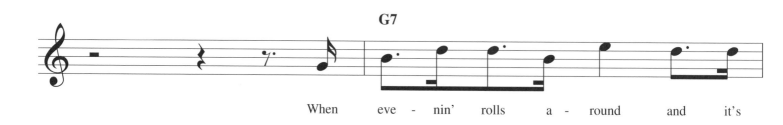

When eve - nin' rolls a - round and it's

time to go to town, where do you go to rock and

roll? The old folks say that you

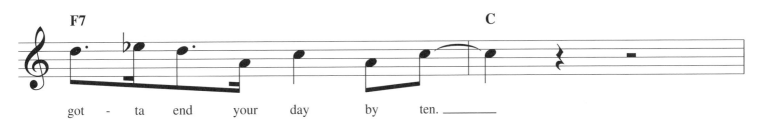

got - ta end your day by ten. _____

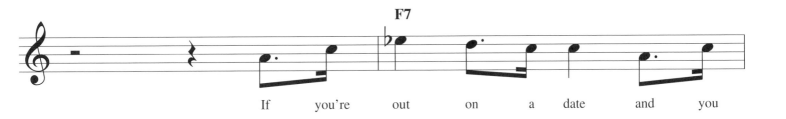

If you're out on a date and you

bring it home late, it's a sin.

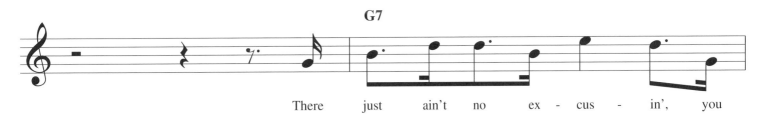

There just ain't no ex - cus - in', you

know you're gon - na lose _____ and nev - er win. _____

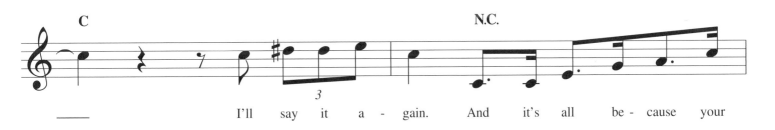

_____ I'll say it a - gain. And it's all be - cause your

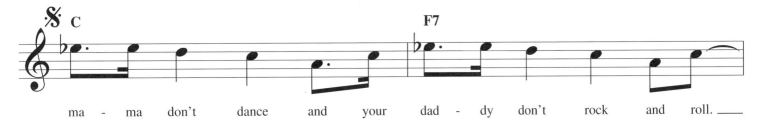

ma - ma don't dance and your dad - dy don't rock and roll. _____

YOU ARE MY SUNSHINE

Words and Music by
JIMMIE DAVIS

The oth - er night, dear, _____ as I lay sleep - ing, _____ I dreamed I
love you _____ and make you hap - py _____ if you will
once, dear, _____ you real - ly loved me _____ and no one

held you in my arms. _____ When I a - woke, dear, _____
on - ly say the same. _____ But if you leave me _____
else could come be - tween. _____ But now you've left me _____

_____ I was mis - tak - en _____ and I hung my head and
_____ to love an - oth - er, _____ you'll re - gret it all some -
_____ and love an - oth - er, _____ you have shat - tered all my

cried: _____
day: _____ } You are my sun - shine, _____ my on - ly sun - shine. _____
dreams: _____

_____ You make me hap - py _____ when skies are gray. _____ You'll nev - er

know, dear, _____ how much I love you. _____ Please don't take my

1, 2 C

3 C

sun - shine a - way. _____ I'll al - ways way. _____
You told me

CHORD SPELLER

C chords

C	C–E–G
Cm	C–E♭–G
C7	C–E–G–B♭
Cdim	C–E♭–G♭
C+	C–E–G♯

C♯ or D♭ chords

C♯	C♯–F–G♯
C♯m	C♯–E–G♯
C♯7	C♯–F– G♯–B
C♯dim	C♯–E–G
C♯+	C♯–F–A

D chords

D	D–F♯–A
Dm	D–F–A
D7	D–F♯–A–C
Ddim	D–F–A♭
D+	D–F♯–A♯

E♭ chords

E♭	E♭–G–B♭
E♭m	E♭–G♭–B♭
E♭7	E♭–G–B♭–D♭
E♭dim	E♭–G♭–A
E♭+	E♭–G–B

E chords

E	E–G♯–B
Em	E–G–B
E7	E–G♯–B–D
Edim	E–G–B♭
E+	E–G♯–C

F chords

F	F–A–C
Fm	F–A♭–C
F7	F–A–C–E♭
Fdim	F–A♭–B
F+	F–A–C♯

F♯ or G♭ chords

F♯	F♯–A♯–C♯
F♯m	F♯–A–C♯
F♯7	F♯–A♯–C♯–E
F♯dim	F♯–A–C
F♯+	F♯–A♯–D

G chords

G	G–B–D
Gm	G–B♭–D
G7	G–B–D–F
Gdim	G–B♭–D♭
G+	G–B–D♯

G♯ or A♭ chords

A♭	A♭–C–E♭
A♭m	A♭–B–E♭
A♭7	A♭–C–E♭–G♭
A♭dim	A♭–B–D
A♭+	A♭–C–E

A chords

A	A–C♯–E
Am	A–C–E
A7	A–C♯–E–G
Adim	A–C–E♭
A+	A–C♯–F

B♭ chords

B♭	B♭–D–F
B♭m	B♭–D♭–F
B♭7	B♭–D–F–A♭
B♭dim	B♭–D♭–E
B♭+	B♭–D–F♯

B chords

B	B–D♯–F♯
Bm	B–D–F♯
B7	B–D♯–F♯–A
Bdim	B–D–F
B+	B–D♯–G

Important Note: A slash chord (C/E, G/B) tells you that a certain bass note is to be played under a particular harmony. In the case of C/E, the chord is C and the bass note is E.

HAL LEONARD PRESENTS
FAKE BOOKS FOR BEGINNERS!

Entry-level fake books! These books feature larger-than-most fake book notation with simplified harmonies and melodies – and all songs are in the key of C. An introduction addresses basic instruction on playing from a fake book.

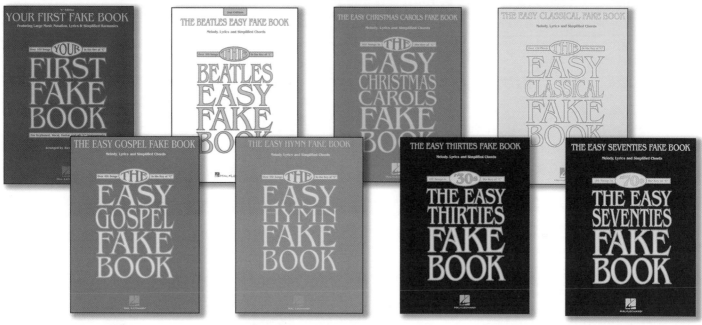

YOUR FIRST FAKE BOOK
00240112...$20.50

THE EASY FAKE BOOK
00240144...$19.99

THE SIMPLIFIED FAKE BOOK
00240168...$19.95

**THE BEATLES EASY
FAKE BOOK – 2ND EDITION**
00171200 ....$25.00

**THE EASY BROADWAY FAKE BOOK –
2ND EDITION**
00276670...$19.99

THE EASY CHILDREN'S FAKE BOOK
00240428 ....$19.99

THE EASY CHRISTIAN FAKE BOOK
00240328...$19.99

**THE EASY CHRISTMAS CAROLS
FAKE BOOK**
00238187 ....$19.99

**THE EASY CHRISTMAS SONGS
FAKE BOOK**
00277913...$19.99

THE EASY CLASSIC ROCK FAKE BOOK
00240389 ....$24.99

THE EASY CLASSICAL FAKE BOOK
00240262...$19.99

THE EASY COUNTRY FAKE BOOK
00240319...$19.99

**THE EASY DISNEY FAKE BOOK –
2ND EDITION**
00275405...$19.99

THE EASY FOLKSONG FAKE BOOK
00240360...$19.99

THE EASY 4-CHORD FAKE BOOK
00118752 ....$19.99

THE EASY G MAJOR FAKE BOOK
00142279 ....$19.99

THE EASY GOSPEL FAKE BOOK
00240169...$19.99

THE EASY HYMN FAKE BOOK
00240207...$19.99

**THE EASY JAZZ STANDARDS
FAKE BOOK**
00102346...$19.99

THE EASY LATIN FAKE BOOK
00240333...$19.99

THE EASY LOVE SONGS FAKE BOOK
00159775 ....$19.99

THE EASY MOVIE FAKE BOOK
00240295...$19.95

THE EASY POP/ROCK FAKE BOOK
00141667 ....$19.99

THE EASY 3-CHORD FAKE BOOK
00240388 ....$19.99

THE EASY WORSHIP FAKE BOOK
00240265...$19.99

**MORE OF THE EASY WORSHIP
FAKE BOOK**
00240362 ....$19.99

THE EASY TWENTIES FAKE BOOK
00240336 ....$19.99

THE EASY THIRTIES FAKE BOOK
00240335...$19.99

THE EASY FORTIES FAKE BOOK
00240252...$19.99

THE EASY FIFTIES FAKE BOOK
00240255...$19.95

THE EASY SIXTIES FAKE BOOK
00240253...$19.99

THE EASY SEVENTIES FAKE BOOK
00240256...$19.99

THE EASY EIGHTIES FAKE BOOK
00240340 ....$19.99

THE EASY NINETIES FAKE BOOK
00240341 ....$19.99

HAL•LEONARD®

www.halleonard.com

*Prices, contents and availability
subject to change without notice.*